D1607644

The Glory of the Cosmos

The Glory
of the
Cosmos

*A Catholic Approach to
the Natural World*

EDITED BY
THOMAS STORCK

AROUCA
PRESS

Copyright © Arouca Press 2020
Introduction © Thomas Storck

Permission has been granted by the individual contributors
for their works to appear in this edited volume.

All rights reserved:
No part of this book may be reproduced or transmitted,
in any form or by any means, without permission

ISBN: 978-1-989905-26-5 (pbk)
ISBN: 978-1-989905-27-2 (hardcover)

Arouca Press
PO Box 55003
Bridgeport PO
Waterloo, ON N2J3G0
Canada
www.aroucapress.com
Send inquiries to info@aroucapress.com

Book and cover design by
Michael Schrauzer

CONTENTS

REFERENCES

Previously published material in this book appeared as follows:

Chapter 2: An earlier version was published in the *Proceedings of the ACPA*, Vol. 85, 2011. Previous versions were read at the Institute for the Study of Nature Summer Conference, M. I. T., June 2008, and the American Catholic Philosophical Association, St. Louis, MO, October 2011.

Chapter 3: Revision of "Reading Natural Hierarchy in a Trinitarian Key." *Communio, International Catholic Review*, vol. XLII, no. 4, Winter 2015, pp. 652–92.

Chapter 4: Revision of a talk originally delivered at World Youth Day 2013, Rio de Janeiro, Brazil, as part of a conference, "Jesus and Nature: Catholic Perspectives on Environmental Issues," sponsored by *Creatio*, a Catholic environmental organization based in Denver, Colorado.

Chapter 5: Originally published in *The Catholic Faith*, vol. 5, no. 6, November/December 1999, pp. 6-12. Slightly revised here.

Chapter 7: Originally published as "The Art of the Spheres: Discovering Mathematical Ideals in Christian Abstract Art," in *Second Spring: International Journal of Faith and Culture*, Issue 8, 2006.

Chapter 8: Originally published in *Second Spring: International Journal of Faith and Culture*, Issue 7, 2006, pp. 33–42.

Chapter 9: Originally appeared in *The Distributist Review*, May 2016. Slightly revised here.

Epilogue: Material in this Epilogue was first published at *New Liturgical Movement*, *LifeSite News*, and *Corpus Christi Watershed*.

INTRODUCTION

THOMAS STORCK

ONE OF THE MOST UNFORTUNATE characteristics of the human mind since the Fall of our first parents is its tendency to run to extremes, to stake out two positions as far as possible from each other, and then to do battle for each position, with little or no recognition that sometimes a middle position, or at least one not on the extremes, is where the truth lies. This is the case with the subject of this book, our treatment of the natural environment in which mankind has been placed by Almighty God. Today we have those who view the natural world as little more than raw material for our use and exploitation, and on the other hand, those who want to attribute some sort of divinity to that world. It is especially unfortunate that tendencies toward both these extremes appear even among Catholics, for it is a fact, albeit not so well known as it should be, that the Church has her own approach to these questions, an approach that, while of course not seeing the natural environment as possessed of divinity, neither does it see it as simply so much inert stuff, stuff meant solely for our manipulation, profit and pleasure.

Those advocating for some kind of pantheistic attitude toward the natural world very often have no real understanding of what a genuine Christian, that is, Catholic, attitude is. Some of them have opted to frankly embrace some kind of paganism. Christianity in their minds is identified with a kind of desiccated and mechanistic deism, opposed to the natural world and to the joys and pleasures of this life.

> The monotheists posit that the Divine is entirely different from Nature, that Nature is a clockwork that the Divine had made like a watchmaker, that the Divine is totally different from Nature, that it is "supernatural." The God of the monotheists is an "owner-operator" of the cosmos.... [1]

---

1 Ian Corrigan, "Discussing Pagan Theology." www.adf.org/articles/cosmology/discussing-pagan-theology.html Accessed July 6, 2020.

Hence, as they see it, the tendency to flee from the things of this life.

> The goal of this old 'sacred game' [of patriarchal religion] is to get away from the ordinary, the natural, the 'unsacred' — away from women, fleshly bodies, decaying nature, away from all that is rooted in mortality and dying. 'Up, up and away' is the cry of this religious consciousness as it seeks to ascend to the elevated realm of pure spirit and utter transcendence where nothing gets soiled, or rots, or dies.[2]

And therefore, paganism is seen as the superior religious option:

> There are religions which celebrate life and others which exalt death as the portico of an eternal life in which, unfortunately, men are deprived of their most natural attributes, those which make us feel joy and happiness in this world, in order to see themselves transformed into wandering spirits whose only allowable delight is to contemplate the Supreme Being.[3]

But the attitude toward the natural world criticized in these quotes is not that of Catholic tradition, a tradition that speaks of the intimate relationship between God and his creation. As St. Thomas Aquinas said, *quod Deus sit in omnibus rebus et intime*, "that God is in all things and most intimately."[4] It is not even correct to say that God is "totally different from Nature," or "wholly other," as a common phrase, repeated often without due consideration, has it.[5] But especially when we contemplate the taking of flesh by the Divine Logos, one could not reasonably say that the God of Catholicism desires to get "away from

2 Elizabeth Dodson Gray, quoted in Cynthia Eller, *Living in the Lap of the Goddess* (New York: Crossroad, c. 1993), p. 136.
3 José Vicente Pascual, "El paganismo: religión de la vida terrenal," *Elementos*, no. 82, p. 76. My translation.
4 *Summa Theologiae*, I, q. 8, a. 1.
5 If God and his attributes can be spoken of analogically, then God is not "wholly other." Indeed, the analogy of being posits that there *are* similarities between God and his creatures, even if the differences are greater, for otherwise we could not speak of an analogy. Cf. *Catechism of the Catholic Church*, no. 41.

women, fleshly bodies, decaying nature, away from all that is rooted in mortality and dying." Quite the contrary.

Nor does Catholic Christianity condemn the pleasures of the body and the joys of this life. Speaking of the thought of St. Thomas Aquinas, Josef Pieper wrote,

> Sensuality [*Sinnlichkeit*] is good (so much so that Thomas calls "unsensuality" not merely a defect, but a *vitium*, a moral deficiency); anger is good; sexuality is good. We might cite hundreds of such sentences. Once Thomas refers to several Fathers of the Church who held that the reproduction of the human race in Paradise must have taken place in some nonsexual manner. With utter calmness, objectivity, but also absolute firmness, St. Thomas replies: *Hoc non dicitur rationabiliter*, "This cannot be said reasonably...."[6]

Pieper sums up Thomas's thought in these words: "What is, is good, because it was created by God; whoever casts aspersions upon the perfection of created things casts aspersions upon the perfection of the divine power."[7]

Of course, this does not mean that according to Catholic thought we can simply accept or embrace without consideration or hesitation any and every desire or pleasure that a human being might find appealing. Mere observation of humanity and its conduct shows us that, as St. John Henry Newman wrote, "the human race is implicated in some terrible aboriginal calamity. It is out of joint with the purposes of its Creator."[8] But this fact does not imply what so many, both our critics and even many Catholics, think. It does not necessitate or imply a negative view of the created world, nor of human nature, nor of the genuine good things of this world.

It is not Catholic thought, then, at least not Catholic Thomistic thought, that was the origin of the point of view that regards nature and the natural with contempt or suspicion. It had its origins in philosophical and religious

6 *Guide to Thomas Aquinas* (Notre Dame: University of Notre Dame, 1987), p. 122.
7 *Ibid.*, p. 131.
8 *Apologia pro Vita Sua* (New York: Modern Library, c. 1950), p. 241.

developments that began in the late Middle Ages, and flowered in the sixteenth century and afterwards. What had its remote causes in philosophical nominalism found a full flowering in the thought of René Descartes and became institutionalized in the presuppositions and methodology of modern science. The mode of inquiry of modern mathematical science, concerned only with those aspects of things which can be quantified, necessarily tends to remove God from an intimate relationship with his creation and finally makes him simply the deistic watchmaker. In the brilliant first chapter of his *English Literature in the Sixteenth Century* C. S. Lewis sketches the progress of mathematical science and its effects on man's relationship with nature.

> What was fruitful in the thought of the new scientists was the bold use of mathematics in the construction of hypotheses, tested not by observation simply but by controlled observation of phenomena that could be precisely measured. On the practical side it was this that delivered Nature into our hands. And on our thoughts and emotions ... it was destined to have profound effects. By reducing Nature to her mathematical elements it substituted a mechanical for a genial or animistic conception of the universe. The world was emptied, first of her indwelling spirits, then of her occult sympathies and antipathies, finally of her colours, smells, and tastes.... The result was dualism rather than materialism. The mind, on whose ideal constructions the whole method depended, stood over against its object in ever sharper dissimilarity. Man, with his new powers became rich like Midas but all that he touched had gone dead and cold. This process, slowly working, ensured during the next century the loss of the old mythical imagination: the conceit, and later the personified abstraction, takes its place. Later still, as a desperate attempt to bridge a gulf which begins to be found intolerable, we have the Nature poetry of the Romantics.[9]

9 *English Literature in the Sixteenth Century* (Oxford: Clarendon Press, 1954), pp. 3–4.

But modern science *must* work by "reducing Nature to her mathematical elements." That is the secret of its power, its power not to know things, but to manipulate them, to understand them only mathematically, to see only one dimension of their reality. Whatever could not be reduced to mathematics was in practice disregarded. It was of no interest to the scientist because his methodology did not know how to deal with it. Thus would seem to follow necessarily that fatal separation of God from nature. "In the process, nature came to be seen as resources to be manipulated and exploited for gain, thus resulting in the industrial revolution and modern capitalism."[10]

In addition to a misunderstanding of the philosophical underpinnings of Catholic thought, there is often an attempt to appeal to Sacred Scripture to support the view that Christianity (of any type) holds an exploitative view of the natural world. It is said that the commandment in Genesis 1:28, "fill the earth and subdue it," constitutes unimpeachable testimony of this exploiting attitude. This was perhaps most famously and cogently expressed in Lynn White's 1967 article, "The Historical Roots of Our Ecologic Crisis."[11] White's article is by no means a crude diatribe and he makes an apparently plausible case for his conclusions, which may be summed up in this passage, "Hence we shall continue to have a worsening ecologic crisis until we reject the Christian axiom that nature has no reason for existence save to serve man."[12] We are entitled to ask, however, whether the Christian tradition as preserved in the Catholic Church does really maintain that "nature has no reason for existence save to serve man." Some of the most beautiful texts in Sacred Scripture, such as Psalm 104 or Daniel 3:35–59 evidence a sensitive appreciation of the natural world, and the latter passage in particular attributes to created beings a definite value besides their utility to mankind, for the heavenly bodies, the animals and the plants are all invoked as

---

10 Terence L. Nichols, *The Sacred Cosmos: Christian Faith and the Challenge of Naturalism* (Grand Rapids: Brazos Press, 2003), p. 9.

11 Published in *Science*, vol. 155, no. 3767, March 10, 1967, pp. 1203-7. Available at www.cmu.ca/faculty/gmatties/lynnwhiterootsofcrisis.pdf Accessed July 23, 2020.

12 *Ibid.*, p. 1207.

existing for the praise of God, quite apart from any use by man.[13] Moreover, in the creation account in the first chapter of Genesis, God repeatedly calls his nascent creation *good*, even before the first human beings are created in verse 27.

Another point made by White also deserves critical attention. He speaks of the momentous nature of the change from desiring to understand to desiring to dominate nature. In this connection White mentions and praises St. Francis of Assisi and Eastern Christian theology, but he takes no notice of the central figure in the Catholic intellectual tradition, Thomas Aquinas. We have already seen Thomas's benign acceptance of creation as proceeding from the hand of God, and moreover he is squarely among those seeking to understand rather than exploit. When White says that "Eastern theology has been intellectualist. Western theology has been voluntarist. The Greek saint contemplates, the Western saint acts,"[14] he is highlighting indeed certain trends in Western Christian thought, but not Thomas himself, for whom the primacy of the intellect over the will is a key point in philosophical anthropology. Latin Christendom did embrace voluntarism after St. Thomas's death, and the eventually triumphant nominalism does indeed appear to have helped prepare the way for Baconian and Cartesian science. And when Thomas again began to be appreciated, beginning in the late fifteenth century, whatever influence his philosophy of nature might have had on the cultural trajectory of Europe was soon overshadowed by the nascent but already powerful scientific revolution.

An additional reason, especially in the United States, for the unthinking assumption that Christianity necessarily fosters an attitude of exploitative dominance toward the natural world, is because of the historic predominance of Protestantism in this country. As a result, Christianity is most often seen through a Protestant lens, even by those who are not themselves believers and who know very well that Protestants are a minority among Christians worldwide, and historical latecomers in addition. For in this as in many other matters,

13   Protestant Bibles omit this passage, which is not in the Masoretic text.
14   White, "Historical Roots," p. 1206.

Americans tend to unthinkingly regard the Protestant tradition as normative. Our university curriculums, for example, pay little attention to southern or eastern European philosophical or political thought, and in matters of religion, the Bible, with the Protestant canon no less, is simply assumed to be the basis of Christianity. Yet Protestant Christianity, at least as much as the philosophical developments previously mentioned, effected a significant change in the way men thought about the created universe. In his well-known work, *The Sacred Canopy*, Peter Berger wrote,

> If we look at these two religious constellations more carefully, though, Protestantism may be described in terms of an immense shrinkage in the scope of the sacred in reality, as compared with its Catholic adversary. The sacramental apparatus is reduced to a minimum and, even there, divested of its more numinous qualities.... At the risk of some simplification, it can be said that Protestantism divested itself as much as possible from the three most ancient and most powerful concomitants of the sacred — mystery, miracle, and magic. This process has been aptly caught in the phrase "disenchantment of the world." The Protestant believer no longer lives in a world ongoingly penetrated by sacred beings and forces. Reality is polarized between a radically transcendent divinity and a radically "fallen" humanity that, *ipso facto*, is devoid of sacred qualities. Between them lies an altogether "natural" universe, God's creation to be sure, but in itself bereft of numinosity.... This reality then became amenable to the systematic, rational penetration, both in thought and in activity, which we associate with modern science and technology.[15]

From such attitudes arise the notion that "[t]he God of the monotheists is an 'owner-operator' of the cosmos." Although Catholics have not always lived up to the demands of their faith, or even seen and understood its implications, its authentic genius has been toward understanding the world of nature

15 Garden City, N.Y.: Doubleday, 1967, pp. III-13.

rather than exploiting it. To be sure, the world *was* created for man's use, but that can be understood in more than one way. Use, of course, is not abuse, but even beyond that point, it is wrong to say that Catholicism saw the created world as existing *exclusively* for man. In addition to the passages from Scripture that I cited above which acknowledge a role for created nature in praise of God entirely separate from their usefulness to humanity, the *Catechism of the Catholic Church* (339) teaches "Each of the various creatures [is] willed in its own being [and] reflects in its own way a ray of God's infinite wisdom and goodness." Moreover St. Thomas's whole doctrine presupposes that the goodness and perfection of individual created things lies in their fulfillment of their own natural tendencies. Thus we may take Lynn White's thesis as applying only with important qualifications to Catholic thought and life.

In fact, the attitude of genuine Catholic thought, based on the natural law and the instincts of humanity, is simply that of traditional cultures in most of the earth, where these have not been destroyed by modernity. Catherine de Hueck Doherty has written eloquently on the attitudes toward the earth and farming that she recalled from her youth in Russia.

> The spade-bearded figure of our farm superintendent of yesteryear rose before me. He was discussing a field with my father who had a farm of 800 arable aces. It had been in our family from sometime since the twelfth century. He was talking to my father about one field in particular. He said it was sick!...
>
> He told my father why this field got sick. It was because we had not put back into it what we had taken away from it. It had grown wheat last year, but there was a new hired man who hadn't put the straw back after the harvest. Earnestly, the peasant (the farm doctor!) kept repeating that the law of fertility of the soil was very simple: You must put back what you took away....
>
> Another long-forgotten memory came back to me at this point as I remembered the spade-bearded man. Now he was discussing with my father another

field that he said was dying. Sleep, he said, would
not restore that field. It had to be healed lovingly
and patiently. They spoke of trees as the remedy....
   Today, in our new world, the earth is treated as
if it were a factory. It is wounded by machines. It
is fed man-made chemicals that produce a large but
far less tasty or healthy crop. It has become almost
a synthetic factory with a production line.[16]

Readers of this volume will find these and other aspects
of this question discussed in considerable detail, from the
standpoints of philosophy, theology, Sacred Scripture and
the liturgy, and as they apply not only to our treatment of
the natural world, but to the economy, and indeed to our
entire way of life. It is the hope of the contributors to this
work that Catholics and others will be able to see that we are
not forced to choose between a dry rationalistic deism and a
revived paganism. May both St. Francis and St. Thomas by
their intercession aid in the restoration of a genuine Catholic
and traditional attitude toward and acceptance of the created
world, the work of the Divine Trinity.

16 Catherine de Hueck Doherty, *Apostolic Farming* (Combermere,
    Ontario: Madonna House, 1991), pp. 2, 4, 6.

I

What are Natural Things?

EDMUND WALDSTEIN, O.CIST.

I WANT TO CONTRAST TWO WAYS OF understanding natural things—one profoundly true, the other dangerously false. The first is exemplified by Aristotle in the 4th century B.C., the other by René Descartes in the 17th century of the Christian era. The disagreement is so general and abstract that it might be thought to be of no practical significance. But the most general and abstract thoughts can have the most far reaching consequences—consequences not only in thought but in life. The relation is, of course, reciprocal; a way of thinking is embodied in a way of life, and life and thought reinforce each other—each makes the other seem obvious and reasonable. I will claim that Descartes's error is at the heart of what Pope Francis has called the "techno-economic paradigm"—the paradigm embodied in modern global capitalism, and all the economic, governmental, technological, scientific, and cultural establishments that rule modern life. The strength of the paradigm means that the error at its heart can seem so obviously true that it does not even require thought. But this error is poisoning the way we treat the earth on which we dwell, our fellow creatures on it, and even ourselves. It is therefore urgently necessary to consider it carefully.

Descartes's error lies in holding that the natural, physical world is most fundamentally *res extensa* quantitative extension, in itself basically featureless and inert, and that all activity and form is imposed on it by extrinsic forces. And, closely connected to this, that the only science worthy of the name is a science that aims at power over the natural world through applying measurement to it.

Before considering this error in detail I will set up a contrast by considering Aristotle's understanding of natural things. Descartes's scientific revolution was in large part an

1

attack on the version of Aristotelianism taught in the schools of his time. And so successful was his polemic that Aristotelianism is most often remembered as a crude caricature of "pre-scientific" thought. But Aristotle actually came to vitally important insights into reality, insights that are in need of recovery if we are to develop an adequate response to the "techno-economic paradigm." And further, these insights were developed and deepened by the greatest scholastic thinker, St. Thomas Aquinas.

COMMON EXPERIENCE AND CONFUSED KNOWLEDGE

Aristotle's greatness as a thinker rests in large part on his patience with the obvious; his willingness to think carefully about the things that we take for granted, and to move slowly forward in thought beginning with them. One must become like a little child, our Lord says, in order to enter the kingdom of Heaven (Matt. 18:3). And the Aristotelian philosopher Duane Berquist remarks that one must similarly have the humility of a little child, the humility to think about the obvious, in order to enter the kingdom of philosophy.[1] Aristotle is a preeminent example of such intellectual humility. He thinks carefully about common experiences, the experiences that we all have and cannot avoid having when we live in this world. The experience of motion would be an example. Everyone who lives in the world experiences things moving and changing, and no one can avoid having that experience. Similarly, we all experience wholes and parts, pleasures and pains, living things and non-living things. Aristotle thinks carefully about such common experiences and about the common notions that our reason naturally receives from such experiences. Hence, the work of philosophy is to make clear what is already contained in the common knowledge of which we speak, to understand it more distinctly, and to make explicit what is implicitly contained in it.[2]

1   Duane Berquist, "Lectures on Ethics," https://archive.org/details/duaneberquistonethics/E003.mp3 Accessed July 3rd, 2020.
2   Cf. Jacob Klein, "Modern Rationalism," in: *Lectures and Essays,* ed. Robert B. Williamson and Elliott Zuckerman (Annapolis: St. John's College Press, 1985), p. 58.

Aristotle makes this clear at the very beginning of his great work on natural philosophy, which we call the *Physics*. He explains that the natural way of proceeding in learning about natural things is to begin with "what are more known and certain to us," and then to proceed to "what are more certain and more knowable by nature." Now, "what are first obvious and certain to us are rather confused," that is, they are a vague and general understanding of things our mind naturally takes in from common experience. Only by a laborious path of thought can we go from that vague knowledge to a more distinct knowledge. And only then can we see the causes standing behind the reality that we experience. It is that knowledge of more primary realities, those upon which other realities depend, that is "what is more certain and more knowable by nature."[3]

An absolutely crucial consequence of this natural path of knowing is that we cannot let a later, more distinct and technical understanding of a thing contradict the more vague and certain knowledge of it. For example, we know in a vague, general, and very certain way that there is a distinction between living and non-living. This follows from our common experience, our immediate contact with reality. Following the natural path, we can come to a more distinct account of what life is. We can also develop criteria for determining in a particular case whether an organism is alive or dead. But it would be absurd if we were to conclude from the more particular investigation that in fact there is no difference between living and non-living, and that a living organism and a non-living organism are both merely arbitrary collections of inert particles acting and reacting to external forces in necessary ways.

NATURE AS AN INTRINSIC PRINCIPLE OF MOTION

In investigating natural things, Aristotle follows the "natural path" to come to an understanding of what natures are. In looking at the world around us we see that some things are natural, and some things artificial. Animals, plants, rivers and rocks come to be "by nature," whereas houses, roads, and

---

3 Aristotle, *Physics*, bk. I, 1; 184a16–20, trans. Glen Coughlin (South Bend: St. Augustine's Press, 2005).

cars are made by human artifice. The word "nature" both in Greek (*physis*), and in Latin (*natura,* from which we derive the English word), is related to the word for birth (*phyein* and *nasci* respectively). Living things are not made from the outside, but come to be from an internal principle of motion. This is true not only of animals like dogs that are "born" in a literal sense, but also, analogously, of plants that come to be from seeds. It is even true, in a weaker sense, of non-living things like rivers and rocks; they are not built by other things. Hence, Aristotle defines nature as an internal principle of motion in a thing.[4] There is something inside a tree, say, on account of which the tree takes in water and light and grows towards a certain complete and flourishing state of being a tree and doing what a tree does.

Nature, Aristotle clarifies, is not any principle of motion that happens to be in a thing (for example, a disease), but rather a principle that is in the thing *fundamentally* and *essentially.* In fact, this fundamental principle of motion and change within a thing is what makes a thing to be what it is. Hence nature also means the "whatness" (quiddity) of a thing, that which makes a thing to be what it is. Different kinds of things have different characteristics and act differently because *what* they are differs.[5] That is, they have different principles of motion, change, or development within them.

Note that this is not true of artificial things. A wooden boat does not have a principle of motion fundamentally and essentially interior to it. A boat is made of different parts, each with its own intrinsic nature, and these parts are related to each other in an extrinsic manner, resulting in a certain common way of acting. But if one buried a boat, and, by chance, something sprouted and grew from it, what sprouted would be a tree, not a boat.[6] Insofar as a boat is a principle of characteristic motion and activity, that principle is not something *intrinsic* to the boat, but is imposed on it from the outside by the shipwright.

---

4 Aristotle, *Physics,* bk. II, 1; 192b20.
5 Cf. Thomas Storck, "Aristotle, Your Garden and Your Body," *Homiletic and Pastoral Review* (February 1993), pp. 24–29, at p. 24.
6 Cf. Aristotle, *Physics,* bk. II, 1; 193a10.

MATTER AND FORM

Natural things come to be and pass away. An animal comes to be by conception, and it passes away when it dies. Coming to be and passing away seem to be changes. But there is a difficulty here. Usually when something changes we see that there is an underlying subject that remains the same, while some characteristic of it passes away and another comes to be. For example, if I blush I have an underlying subject (my face) in which white color passes away and red color comes to be. Or if I grow there is an underlying subject (me), in which one determination (smaller size) passes away and another determination (larger size) comes to be. But in the case of a whole natural *thing* coming to be there does not seem to be any subject underlying the change. A dog is a thing, not a determination of something else. When a dog dies, there is no thing that was first a dog and then not a dog.

Aristotle solves this difficulty by arguing that natural things are composed of what he calls "matter" and "form." Or, more precisely, "prime matter" and "substantial form." Prime matter is an underlying subject that never exists in its own right, but only exists as what underlies a thing. Prime matter is the *ability* or *potential* to be a thing, but it is not (on Aristotle's account) itself a thing. Substantial form is what *makes a thing to be what it is.* Substantial form never exists on its own, but only as it informs some determining matter. A natural thing is prime matter determined by substantial form. A natural thing is *one single thing,* the union of matter and form. When a dog is conceived the form of a dog is coming to be in the matter where the form of sperm and ovum were before; when a dog dies its matter assumes the forms of the various chemical elements formerly integrated by and into the nature of the dog, but that now go their separate ways, so to speak.

NATURE ACTS FOR AN END

Matter is the potential or ability for form. Aristotle can therefore say that matter is *for the sake of form.* That is, matter has a purpose that is fulfilled when it is "actualized" by form. At times, Aristotle even speaks of matter *desiring* form.[7] In its most basic principles, therefore, nature is *purposive, teleological;* it is aiming at something good. Aristotle argues that this purposiveness of nature characterizes all natural activity. Nature is an intrinsic principle of motion, and this motion is aimed at the fullness of being and activity of a natural thing. When a tree grows and stretches out its branches it is doing so for the sake of a purpose, for the full actualization of tree-nature, the perfection of tree-life. This purposiveness of natural activity is not random, nor by chance, it is a stable inclination within natural things. Aristotle manifests this by a comparison of nature to human activities which help nature along. In medicine, for example, the physician helps nature to achieve the healing that it was already striving to gain.

The purposiveness of nature, Aristotle maintains, is most manifest in natural things that go through a set of ordered actions, terminating in something beneficial to them. For example, a spider goes through a set sequence of actions to spin a web, a web which ends up being useful to the spider. There appears to be something almost like intelligence in the spider's actions. "Whence some people are at a loss as to whether spiders and ants and such things work by mind or by something else."[8] And yet, spiders clearly do not act by deliberating or planning in their *own* minds. They act instinctively. There seems, therefore, to be a wisdom in the purposiveness of natural things that is not the wisdom of their own minds.

NATURES AS DIVINE WORDS

St. Thomas Aquinas takes this Aristotelian account and develops it further. He argues that to act for an end necessarily presupposes some kind of intelligence. So, he argues, natures are, as it were, impressions of the Divine intelligence on creatures; the nature of each thing is a participation in the divine wisdom by which that thing is directed towards its end:

7 *Ibid.,* bk. I, 9; 191a20–23.
8 *Ibid.,* bk. II, 8; 199a21.

For nature seems to differ from art only because nature is an intrinsic principle and art is an extrinsic principle. For if the art of ship building were intrinsic to wood, a ship would have been made by nature in the same way as it is made by art... Hence, it is clear that nature is nothing but the reason (*ratio*) of a certain kind of art, i.e., the divine art, impressed upon things, by which these things are moved to a determinate end. It is as if the shipbuilder were able to give to timbers that by which they would move themselves to take the form of a ship.[9]

The Thomist philosopher Charles De Koninck in commenting on this passage says that every nature can be called a "Divine *logos* . . . a Divine word"[10] *Logos* can of course mean *reason* as well as word and De Koninck notes that the nature of irrational things is "a substitute for intelligence,"[11] but a nature is also a word in a more literal sense. God's principal intention in creating is to manifest his own glory, and so each nature is a sign by which God leads rational creatures to a knowledge of himself. As St. Thomas puts it:

The creatures made by God's wisdom are related to God's wisdom, whose signposts they are, as a man's words are related to his wisdom, which they signify. And just as a disciple reaches an understanding of the teacher's wisdom by the words he hears from him, so man can teach an understanding of God's wisdom by examining the creatures he made.[12]

In coming to know the natures of things, therefore, we come to know the Creator, who inscribed those natures in things.

---

9   St. Thomas Aquinas, *Commentary on Aristotle's Physics*, lectio 14, 268; Cf. Pope Francis, *Laudato si'*, no. 80.
10   Charles De Koninck, *The Principle of the New Order*, in: *The Writings of Charles De Koninck,* vol. 2, trans. Ralph McInerny (Notre Dame: University of Notre Dame Press, 2009), p. 143.
11   *Ibid.*
12   St. Thomas Aquinas, *Commentary on 1 Corinthians*, Lectio 3, 55.

PREMODERN SCIENCE, CULTURE, AND ECONOMY

For Aristotle, as for most ancient and medieval thinkers, the study of nature, natural philosophy or natural science, is primarily a contemplative activity done for its own sake, a "looking" at the truth without ulterior motive. As Jacob Klein, the great philosopher and historian of science, put it:

> In Greek *episteme* [science] the life of "cognition" and "knowledge" was recognized for the first time as an ultimate human possibility, one which enables men to disregard all the ends they might otherwise pursue, to devote themselves to contemplation in complete freedom and leisure, and to find their happiness in this very activity. This possibility is contrasted with the bondage imposed by the affairs of the day.[13]

The contemplation of natural things led ultimately to the contemplation of the divine first cause of all things, the knowledge of whom is happiness. Of course, the ancients recognized that knowledge of natural things has practical applications, but these applications were seen as being of secondary importance. Thus Plutarch, in the life of Marcellus, recounts that Archimedes, who had invented many powerful engines of war for the defense of Syracuse, left no designs of them behind in writing, for,

> repudiating as sordid and ignoble the whole trade of engineering, and every sort of art that lends itself to mere use and profit, he placed his whole affection and ambition in those purer speculations where there can be no reference to the vulgar needs of life; studies, the superiority of which to all others is unquestioned.[14]

If the philosophers scorned practical pursuits, it is nonetheless the case that their understanding of natural things as having intrinsic principles of motion, ordered to an end, was

13 Jacob Klein, *Greek Mathematical Thought and the Origin of Algebra*, trans. Eva Brann (New York: Dover, 1992), p. 118.
14 Plutarch, *The Lives of the Noble Grecians and Romans*, vol. 1, (New York: The Modern Library, 1992), p. 420.

reflected in the practical life and culture of their times: in the cultivation of the earth, in the production and exchange of goods, in the understanding of personal virtue, and in politics. In all these areas it was presumed that man ought to work with the grain of natures.

Of course, culture includes modifying nature in some ways to make it more useful to human purposes, for example, by domesticating plants and animals, building cities, etc. But in all this a certain respect for natural tendencies was manifest. Consider, for example, an anonymous twelfth century description of St. Bernard's abbey of Clairvaux. The anonymous author waxes lyrical about the beauty of the cultivated vineyards and orchards which from the labor of the monks has turned into a source of abundance. He is particularly taken by the great water-works that monks constructed:

> This water, which serves the dual purpose of feeding the fish and irrigating the vegetables, is supplied by the tireless course of the river Aube, of famous name, which flows through the many workshops of the abbey. Wherever it passes it evokes a blessing in its wake, proportionate to its good offices; for it does not slip through unscathed or at its leisure, but at the cost of much exertion. By means of a winding channel cut through the middle of the valley, not by nature but by the hard work of the brethren, the Aube sends half its waters into the monastery, as though to greet the monks [...] As much of the stream as this wall, acting as gatekeeper, allows in by the sluice-gates hurls itself initially with swirling force against the mill, where its ever-increasing turbulence, harnessed first to the weight of the mill-stones and next to the fine-meshed sieve, grinds the grain and then separates the flour from the bran. [...] O Lord, how great are the consolations that you in your goodness provide for your poor servants, lest a greater wretchedness engulf them! How generously you palliate the hardships of your penitents, lest perchance they be crushed at times by the harshness of their toil! From how much back-breaking travail for horses and arm-aching labour for men

9

does this obliging torrent free us, to the extent that
without it we should be neither clothed nor fed. It
is most truly shared with us, and expects no other
reward wheresoever it toils under the sun than that,
its work done, it be allowed to run freely away.[15]

In his *Letters from Lake Como* Romano Guardini, reflects
on how the Italian landscape, with its vineyards and villages,
is shaped by a kind of culture that certainly modifies nature,
but in a way that stays close to natural purposes:

> As I walked through the valleys of Brianza, from
> Milan to Lake Como, luxuriant, cultivated with zeal-
> ous industry, encircled by austere mountains, broad
> and powerful, I could not believe my eyes. Every-
> where it was an inhabited land, valleys and slopes
> dotted with hamlets and small towns. All nature had
> been given a new shape by us humans. What culture
> means in its narrowest sense struck me with full
> force. The lines of the roofs merged from different
> directions. They went through the small town set
> on the hillside or followed the windings of a val-
> ley. Integrated in many ways, they finally reached
> a climax in the belfry with its deep-toned bell. All
> these things were caught up and encircled by the
> well-constructed mountain masses. Culture, very
> lofty and yet self-evident, very naturally — I have no
> other word. Nature, then, has been reshaped, sub-
> jected to mind and spirit, yet it is perfectly simple.
> As I have seen again and again, this is how culture
> as this reshaping affects the conduct of a very simple
> person in both word and behavior, though he or
> she may have no particular self-awareness of this. It
> is part of such a person's blood and development,
> the legacy of a thousand-year-old process in which
> culture has developed naturally.[16]

---

15 "A Description of Clairvaux," in: *The Cistercian World: Monastic
Writings of the Twelfth Century,* trans. Pauline Matarasso (London:
Penguin, 1993), pp. 287–292, at pp. 288–89.

16 Romano Guardini, *Letters from Lake Como: Explorations on Technology and the Human Race* trans. Geoffrey W. Bromiley (Grand Rapids:
Eerdmans, 1994), p. 5.

At one point he describes seeing a sailboat on Lake Como, and marvels at the way in which intelligence and nature harmonize in sailing:

> It is full of mind and spirit, this perfectly fashioned movement in which we master the force of nature. Certainly, we pay for it already with a certain remoteness. We are no longer plunged into the sphere of wind and water as birds and fishes are. [...] We have both withdrawn from nature and mastered it. Our relation to it is now cooler and more alien. Only in this way can any work of culture, of mind and spirit, be done. Yet do you not see how natural the work remains? The lines and proportions of the ship are still in profound harmony with the pressure of the wind and waves and the vital human measure. Those who control this ship are still very closely related to the wind and waves. They are breast to breast with their force. Eye and hand and whole body brace against them. We have here real culture — elevation above nature, yet decisive nearness to it. We are still in a vital way body, but we are shot through with mind and spirit. We master nature by the power of mind and spirit, but we ourselves remain natural.[17]

In such a culture man is not seen as standing apart from other natural things, but as being one of the natural things of this world, albeit the highest. Hence in every area of life, man is meant to act to fulfill the teleological tendencies of his nature.

DESCARTES'S REVOLUTION

Descartes's scientific revolution was certainly prepared by various developments both in science and in life. Late medieval nominalism had weakened the teleological understanding of nature. Moreover, the "scholastic" philosophy of the medieval universities had a tendency to become calcified and bookish. While Aristotle had spent a great amount of time in

17 *Ibid.*, pp. 11–12.

careful observation of nature,[18] many scholastic philosophers (though not all) did natural philosophy from the library and the study, without bothering to observe natural things. And this fed into the problem of "sedimentation" or "calcification" of scientific language. The language of natural philosophy came to be an ever more technical language, divorced from the common experience of reality expressed in ordinary speech. Instead of deriving their meaning from common conceptions of experienced reality, the technical terms received their meaning from their relation to other terms in a conceptual system.[19] Scholastic natural philosophy at the time of Descartes was, therefore, only imperfectly Aristotelian.

More practical developments also helped make Descartes's revolution possible. As Charles Taylor has argued, the achievements of social discipline in bringing "civility" to the general population in the period following the Reformation (for example in Calvinist Geneva), and the increased military power and economic productivity that resulted from this achievement, brought about a new sense that man's state could be progressively bettered — this is the beginning of the modern idea of progress.[20] The rise of mercantilism, the beginning of the great transformation of economic life, was already preparing a culture that would find Descartes plausible.[21]

Most important were of course those other thinkers of Descartes's time whom we associate with the scientific revolution. As Klein argues, the other pioneers of early modern science such as Simon Stevin (1548–1620), Francis Bacon (1561–1626), and Galileo Galilei (1564–1642), shared a basic orientation with Descartes himself (1596–1650). They were interested in science not primarily as a contemplative activity,

18 See: Armand Marie Leroi, *The Lagoon: How Aristotle Invented Science* (New York: Viking, 2014).

19 Cf. Klein, "Modern Rationalism," pp. 6–7; cf. Charles De Koninck, "Three Sources of Philosophy," *Proceedings of the American Catholic Philosophical Association* 38 (1964), pp. 13–22.

20 See: Charles Taylor, *A Secular Age* (Cambridge: Belknap Press, 2007), ch. 2.

21 See, Richard W. Hadden, *On the Shoulders of Merchants: Exchange and the Mathematical Conception of Nature in Early Modernity* (Albany: State University of New York Press, 1994).

but as a means of answering practical questions—questions of "applied mechanics and applied optics," questions of how to improve artillery, bridge building, perspective painting, and new optical instruments such as the telescope.[22] Science was for them not primarily a contemplation of the truth, but a *method* or *art* of finding useful truths: "modern science is not so much the understanding of nature as the art of mastering nature."[23] Moreover, they understood that to achieve mastery over nature it was necessary to apply mathematics to the natural world. This had indeed been understood by the ancients as well, who applied mathematics, for example, to levers.[24]

But ancient mathematics was not well suited to mechanical application. It was a contemplative discipline, ordered to the understanding of form. If one compares the laboriousness of the mechanical demonstrations in Galileo's *Discourses on Two New Sciences* (1638) with the simplicity of those in Newton's *Principia* (1687), one can see that a great transformation in mathematics has taken place. Between these two works lies Descartes's *Geometry* (1637). The *Geometry* is a short work that Descartes published as an appendix to the *Discourse on Method,* but it had tremendous influence. According to John Stuart Mill, Descartes's *Geometry* "constitutes the greatest single step ever made in the progress of the exact sciences."[25] Descartes's aim was to homogenize the object of mathematics by uniting geometry and arithmetic, and to revolutionize the method of mathematics "by making the central activity the

---

22   Klein, *Greek Mathematical Thought,* p. 119.
23   Klein, "Modern Rationalism," p. 60.
24   See, Pseudo Aristotle, *Mechanics,* 847a10–28. This text had a great influence on Galileo, who quotes it in his *Discourses on Two New Sciences,* and it was of decisive importance to Francis Bacon. Bacon found in the *Mechanica* the path to be followed in order to find a new science that would give power over nature: "Aristotle has well remarked that Physic and Mathematic produce Practice or Mechanic." Francis Bacon, *The Advancement of Knowledge,* 3.6, in *The Works of Francis Bacon,* ed. James Spedding et al., vol. 4, (London: Longman, 1858) p. 369.
25   John Stuart Mill, *An Examination of William Hamilton's Philosophy and of the Principal Philosophical Questions Discussed in his Writings* (London: Longmans, 1865), p. 531; cf. I. Bernard Cohen, *Revolution in Science* (Cambridge, MA: Belknap, 1985), p. 156.

manipulative working of the mind rather than its visualizing of form."[26]

Descartes's new mathematics was applied to physical reality through measurement, giving rise to a kind of natural science that regarded physical things as undifferentiated quantities. The Aristotelian study of nature was not mathematical, because for Aristotle mathematics does not consider the being of things *as things*, but only the "how much" of things in abstraction from those things.[27] The contemplation of mathematical form in Greek mathematics was rather thought of as propaedeutic to a contemplation of substantial form, the whatness considered in natural philosophy. This whole mode of study is rejected by Descartes. In order to show that his quantitative/algebraic mode of inquiry is the universal science, Descartes develops a new theory of natural being that makes claims that it *is ontologically* nothing more than homogenous quantity. As Klein puts it:

> Descartes' great idea now consists of identifying, by means of "methodological" considerations, the "general" object of this *mathesis universalis* which can be represented and conceived only symbolically — with the "substance" of the world, with corporeality as "extensio." Only by virtue of this identification did symbolic mathematics gain that fundamental position in the system of knowledge which it has never since lost.[28]

And in a note he adds:

> *This* was the issue which compelled Descartes to develop his metaphysics, a metaphysics in which, to be sure, the actual points of departure of his "system" came to be increasingly consigned to oblivion.[29]

Of course, there were other motives that lead Descartes to

---

26 Harvey Flaumenhaft, "Why We Won't Let You Speak of the Square Root of Two," *St. John's Review*, vol. 48, no. 1, 2004, at pp. 7–41 40–41.

27 See, Aristotle, *Physics*, bk. II, 2; 193b 22.

28 Klein, *Greek Mathematical Thought*, p. 197.

29 *Ibid.*, p. 294, note 308; emphasis in original.

formulate his new metaphysics (including the desire to refute Montaigne's skepticism[30]), but the *main* purpose was to justify the place of his new method as *the* universal science.[31]

Already, in his early correspondence with Isaac Beeckman, Descartes had begun to formulate a metaphysics that would homogenize all of corporeal reality. But it was not until he hit upon the famous method of universal doubt inaugurated in the *Discourse on Method* and perfected in the *Meditations on First Philosophy* (1641), that he found a satisfactory rhetorical basis for this system. The foundation of Descartes's method of doubt is a reversal of the Aristotelian teaching on the relative certainty of the confused and the distinct. While for Aristotle what is most certain is the vague, indistinct grasp of the reality that we experience, for Descartes the exact opposite is the case. For Descartes only "clear and distinct" ideas are certain. Vagueness and uncertainty are correlative. Descartes is thinking here above all of the clarity of mathematic ideas, which, since they are abstracted from matter and motion can be clearly seen in the imagination. The result is that he can doubt the evidence of his senses, since sense impressions always lack mathematical clarity. He can therefore also doubt the very existence of the external world, and even of his own body. It is only when it comes to his own existence that he finds he cannot doubt: *cogito ergo sum.* The point of certainty that Descartes finds is thus entirely subjective and interior; he has found the existence of a "thinking thing." He then proceeds to try to find a way to derive certainty about other things from this primal certitude. He does this through an ontological proof for the existence of God, who, he then argues, cannot be deceiving us through our senses; the sensible world therefore exists. The relation of the thinking thing to the extrinsic world, whose existence he has proved by this circuitous route, is of course entirely extrinsic; the outside

30 See, Alasdair MacIntyre, *God, Philosophy, Universities: A Selective History of the Catholic Philosophical Tradition* (Plymouth: Rowman and Littlefield, 2009) chaps. 13–14.

31 Cf. Richard Kennington, *On Modern Origins: Essays in Early Modern Philosophy*, ed. Pamela Krauss and Frank Hunt (Lanham: Lexington, 2004), esp. chaps. 6–7.

world becomes the featureless *res extensa* (extended thing), the object of Cartesian mathematics. This Cartesian world is totally lacking in "natures" as intrinsic principles of motion toward an end. It is without purpose, and without any interior activity. All motion is seen as the effect of external forces. This world does not even have any of the qualities known to our senses—color, taste, fragrance, and sound, are all reduced to the measurable movement of featureless particles. They are illusions engendered in us by matter in motion.

The human person, as the thinking thing, is no longer a part of the natural world. The world becomes a mere object to be dominated.

DESCARTES'S POISON

The program of the domination of nature through Cartesian science destroys the sense of human culture as working with the grain of natures. We can see this, for example, in the cultivation of the earth. As Thomas Storck put it:

> The technological application of Cartesian philosophy to the soil has produced modern chemical farming, farming which is destroying the soil's own nature and treating it as something merely passive, an inert medium which is necessary to make the plants stand up, but which does not supply anything essential for their growth, for the nutrients are now supplied from the outside, i.e., via chemicals. The soil's own rich microbiological life is destroyed and it becomes more and more the undifferentiated stuff we treat it as.[32]

Certainly, the use of synthetic nitrogen fertilizers has vastly increased global food harvests,[33] but at what cost?

In *Letters from Lake Como* Guardini remarks on how the beauty of the landscape, cultivated for centuries in a manner close to nature, is being destroyed by the "machines from the North," where the Cartesian revolution was continued and

32 Thomas Storck, "Aristotle, Your Garden and Your Body," pp. 26–27.
33 See: Vaclav Smil, *Enriching the Earth: Fritz Haber, Carl Bosch, and the Transformation of World Food Production* (Cambridge: The MIT Press, 2001).

embodied in the industrial revolution:

> I saw machines invading the land that had previously been the home of culture. I saw death overtaking a life of infinite beauty, and I felt that this was not just an external loss that we could accept and remain who we were. Instead, a life, a life of supreme value that can arise only in the world that we have long since lost, was beginning to perish here, as well as in the North.[34]

He notes the shock of seeing the Italian landscape marred by a modern factory building:

> Yet all at once, then, on the singing lines of a small town, I saw the great box of a factory. Look how in a landscape in which all the risings and fallings and measures and proportions came together in one clear melody, along with the lofty bell tower there was suddenly a smokestack, and everything fell apart. [...] I have a plain sense that a world is developing in which human beings in this specific sense can no longer live — a world that is in some way nonhuman.[35]

He goes on to contrast the sail-boat with the motor-boat typical of the Cartesian world:

> In the sailing ship we had a natural existence, for all the presence of mind and spirit in the situation. We had our being in a natural culture. In the modern steamer, however, we are in an artificial situation; measured by the vital elastic human limits, nature has been decisively eliminated.[36]

In economic life the Cartesian spirit is melded with the spirit of acquisitiveness. Economic growth is pursued as if for its own sake. In consumerist culture, products are not developed because of their usefulness for the living of a given conception of the good life; on the contrary, bogus images

34 Guardini, *Letters from Lake Como*, p. 5.
35 *Ibid.*, pp. 6–7.
36 *Ibid.*, pp. 13–14.

of the good life are invented by advertisers in order to create the "need" for ever new products.

In modern sexual ethics, too, we see the Cartesian emancipation from natural teleology, and the separation of the human self from the body in full display. The body is seen as an object of domination for the sake of the pleasure or expression of the self, conceived implicitly as the Cartesian "thinking thing."[37]

This is the "technocratic paradigm" decried by Pope Francis. If it is to be overcome, a great deal must be done at all levels. Habits of acting must be changed, but also habits of thinking. One way in which our thinking must change, is that we must recover a more Aristotelian understanding of natural things.

---

37 See: Michael Waldstein, *Glory of the Logos in the Flesh: Saint John Paul's Theology of the Body* (Ave Maria: Sapientia Press, 2020).

2

Brother Wolf or Robo-Dog?

ARE ANIMALS JUST COMPUTERS?

MICHAEL HECTOR STORCK

L ET ME BEGIN WITH A STORY TOLD ABOUT St. Francis of Assisi.

At the time when St Francis was living in the city of Gubbio, a large wolf appeared in the neighbourhood, so terrible and so fierce, that he not only devoured other animals, but made a prey of men also; and since he often approached the town, all the people were in great alarm, and used to go about armed, as if going to battle. Notwithstanding these precautions, if any of the inhabitants ever met him alone, he was sure to be devoured, as all defence was useless: and, through fear of the wolf, they dared not go beyond the city walls. St Francis, feeling great compassion for the people of Gubbio, resolved to go and meet the wolf, though all advised him not to do so. Making the sign of the holy cross, and putting all his confidence in God, he went forth from the city, taking his brethren with him; but these fearing to go any further, St Francis bent his steps alone toward the spot where the wolf was known to be, while many people followed at a distance, and witnessed the miracle. The wolf, seeing all this multitude, ran towards St Francis with his jaws wide open. As he approached, the saint, making the sign of the cross, cried out: "Come hither, brother wolf; I command thee, in the name of Christ, neither to harm me nor anybody else." Marvellous to tell, no sooner had St Francis made the sign of the cross, than the terrible wolf, closing his jaws, stopped running, and coming up to St Francis, lay down at his feet as meekly as a lamb.

19

And the saint thus addressed him: "Brother wolf, thou hast done much evil in this land, destroying and killing the creatures of God without his permission; yea, not animals only hast thou destroyed, but thou hast even dared to devour men, made after the image of God; for which thing thou art worthy of being hanged like a robber and a murderer. All men cry out against thee, the dogs pursue thee, and all the inhabitants of this city are thy enemies; but I will make peace between them and thee, O brother wolf, if so be thou no more offend them, and they shall forgive thee all thy past offences, and neither men nor dogs shall pursue thee any more." Having listened to these words, the wolf bowed his head, and, by the movements of his body, his tail, and his eyes, made signs that he agreed to what St Francis said. On this St Francis added: "As thou art willing to make this peace, I promise thee that thou shalt be fed every day by the inhabitants of this land so long as thou shalt live among them; thou shalt no longer suffer hunger, as it is hunger which has made thee do so much evil; but if I obtain all this for thee, thou must promise, on thy side, never again to attack any animal or any human being; dost thou make this promise?" Then the wolf, bowing his head, made a sign that he consented. Said St Francis again: "Brother wolf, wilt thou pledge thy faith that I may trust to this thy promise?" and putting out his hand he received the pledge of the wolf; for the latter lifted up his paw and placed it familiarly in the hand of St Francis, giving him thereby the only pledge which was in his power. Then said St Francis, addressing him again: "Brother wolf, I command thee, in the name of Christ, to follow me immediately, without hesitation or doubting, that we may go together to ratify this peace which we have concluded in the name of God"; and the wolf, obeying him, walked by his side as meekly as a lamb, to the great astonishment of all the people.[1]

---

1 *The Little Flowers of Saint Francis of Assisi*, Chapter XXI, Of the Most Holy Miracle of St. Francis in Taming the Fierce Wolf of Gubbio.

In the modern imagination, the difference between a complex machine such as a computer and a living thing such as a dog — or wolf — is merely one of degree. No longer will a holy man address an animal as his brother or extract a promise of peace from it, for it is only a machine. Indeed, it is only a matter of time, so it is thought, before technology advances to the point where the mechanical artifact, the robot dog, say, is indistinguishable from, or even surpasses in ability, the natural living being. This is true not only in films or in works of science fiction. Not a few scientists (and many philosophers) talk as if, in essence, living things and mechanisms are not really different.

For example, in 2000, physicist Evelyn Fox Keller made a number of comparisons between living things and computer systems in *The Century of the Gene,* and then asks how they differ. Her only answer is that "computers . . . are built by human design, while organisms evolved without the benefit of a designer (or so it is generally presumed)." In 1966, biochemist John Kendrew stated: "Personally I do not think there is . . . any difference in essence between the living and the non-living, and I think most molecular biologists would share this view."[2]

This mechanical view of living beings has, moreover, had some astounding practical successes. Artificial hearts, organ transplants, immunizations, and the whole science of genetics are only a few of the powerful results of treating living things as nothing more than ordered aggregates. Scientists can explain and manipulate all beings, living and non-living, as if they were only collections of atoms, molecules, and other material parts. So if we grant the success of modern science at explaining and controlling natural things — and this success is undeniable — perhaps the achievements of science, both practical and theoretical, can only be accounted for by a real, hard-headed, and unromantic grasp of the truth about the natural world; perhaps the natural world is simply nothing other than a complex system or structure of elements and particles. If this is the case, then the premodern tradition of natural philosophy, which treats a living thing as having real unity and the whole as prior to its parts, and which includes such seemingly useless baggage as substantial forms and final causes, is an outmoded absurdity, refuted and false.

Furthermore, the view that all things are only arrangements of parts is sometimes thought to have the support of physics. Does not physics explain all visible macroscopic things in terms of atomic elements and sub-atomic particles, down to the level of quarks (and whatever more elementary particles future physicists may discover)? And biology is often — though perhaps more often by philosophers than by biologists — presented as nothing more than an extension of physics to very complex carbon-based systems.[3]

2 Evelyn Fox Keller, *The Century of the Gene* (Cambridge, Mass.: Harvard University Press, 2000), p. 130; John Kendrew, *The Thread of Life: An Introduction to Molecular Biology* (Cambridge Mass., Harvard University Press, 1966), p. 91.
3 See, for example, J. L. Dowell, "Formulating the Thesis of Physicalism:

We do, however, have two very serious reasons for questioning the mechanical or mechanistic view of animals and even plants. The first reason is based on our own experience as knowers. Considered from this point of view, an internal point of view, as it were, it seems obvious that each of us is one thing, and that our experiences of pain or vision cannot wholly be explained by the physical makeup of our bodies, understood as mere collections of particles, molecules, cells, and organs. How can the motion of ions in neurons ever conceivably explain the sight of a red sunset or the sensation of pain in a stubbed toe? Not only *do we not currently have* physical explanations of these things, but, as Thomas Nagel says, "We have at present *no conception* of what an explanation of the physical nature of a mental phenomenon *would be.*"[4] Not only can we not explain sight, for example, solely in terms of the operation of neurons and chemicals, but we do not even know how one would go about formulating such an explanation. Furthermore, if we are only collections of material parts, then it seems impossible for us to have any real knowledge of the world around us. For one thing, it would be unclear what it would mean to say "I." And if there is no *I*, then *I* cannot possibly know anything about biochemistry, nor can *I* meaningfully say things such as "I know" or "I think." For another thing, if the functioning of our brains can be explained entirely in terms of the laws of physics, and thought is entirely determined by our brains, then it seems that all our beliefs and all our reasoning—including scientific reasoning—are determined by the interaction of the molecules and neurons composing our brains. But if our beliefs can be fully explained by the functioning of our brains, then our beliefs do not seem to be the result of our reasoning, but rather of our brain states. And if our beliefs are not the result of our reasoning, then we have no *reason* to believe them. So ultimately, a denial of our own unity denies both the possibility

An Introduction," *Philosophical Studies* 131 (2006): pp. 1–23; J.J.C. Smart, "Materialism," *Journal of Philosophy* 60 (1963): pp. 651–661.
4   Thomas Nagel, "What is it Like to Be a Bat?" in *Modern Philosophy of Mind*, ed. William Lyons (London: J. M. Dent, 1995; reprint, 1999), p. 159, emphasis added.

of the biochemist as possessed of biochemical knowledge and the existence of biochemistry as a truth-seeking endeavor.[5]
    The second reason for questioning the mechanistic model is based on physics. Start with an atom: While a mechanistic view would imagine an atom as a miniature solar system, with relatively small and light electrons orbiting a relatively massive nucleus like planets orbiting a star, this model, plausible as it might seem, cannot accurately reflect the way an atom really is. In *Physics and Beyond: Encounters and Conversations,* Werner Heisenberg recalls a conversation with Niels Bohr, who explains the impossibility of such a mechanical atom:

> My starting point was not at all the idea that an atom is a small-scale planetary system and as such governed by the laws of astronomy. I never took things as literally as that. My starting point was rather the stability of matter, a pure miracle when considered from the standpoint of classical physics.
>
> By 'stability' I mean that the same substances always have the same properties, that the same crystals recur, the same chemical compounds, etc. In other words, even after a host of changes due to external influences, an iron atom will always remain an iron atom, with exactly the same properties as before. This cannot be explained by the principles of classical mechanics, certainly not if the atom resembles a planetary system. Nature clearly has a tendency to produce certain forms — I use the word 'forms' in the most general sense — and to recreate these forms even when they are disturbed or destroyed. You may even think of biology: the stability of living organisms, the propagation of the most complicated forms which, after all, can exist only in their entirety.... All this, far from being self-evident, is quite inexplicable in terms of the basic principle of Newtonian physics, according to which all effects have precisely determined causes, and according to which the present state of

5   St. Thomas Aquinas, *Summa Theologiae,* I, q. 78, a. 1; C. S. Lewis, *Miracles: A Preliminary Study,* revised ed. (1960; reprint, San Francisco: HarperCollins, 2001), chap. 3.

a phenomenon or process is fully determined by the
one that immediately preceded it.[6]

Thus an atom, because of its stability, must be a real whole
and its parts, as parts of the atom, must in some way depend
on that whole, which cannot simply be explained by its parts.
We can illustrate this clearly by looking at a single atom
of, for example, hydrogen. Imagine that a hydrogen atom is
nothing other than a collection of parts, a negatively charged
electron moving around a positively charged nucleus. According to Maxwell's theory of electromagnetism, an accelerating
charged body will emit energy in the form of electromagnetic
radiation. (This is why electrons moving through the wire
of an antenna generate radio waves and why a rotating mag-
net can generate electricity.) Since the electron is negatively
charged, if it orbits the nucleus it will emit radiation and
thus lose energy, slow down, and be attracted to the positively charged nucleus. In other words, the electron cannot
orbit, because if it did, the atom would collapse. If the electron, rather than orbiting, were merely to stay in one place
relative to the positively charged nucleus, it would also be
attracted to the nucleus, and the atom would also collapse.
But if the electron, existing in a state of actuality, moved in
some more complex way, it would either continue in a straight
line and leave the atom, in which case the atom would not
even contain the electron, or else it would eventually have to
turn around, and this, again, would produce electromagnetic
radiation, so that the electron would lose energy and collapse.
There is, then, no way for an atom to contain an electron, if
the electron is an actually existing particle, a mechanical part
which at all times has definite position and velocity.[7]

But since atoms do contain electrons, this can only be the
case if the parts of atoms, protons, neutrons, and electrons,
do not exist as independent entities; mechanical explanations,

6 Werner Heisenberg, *Physics and Beyond: Encounters and Conversations,*
   trans. Arnold J. Pomerans (NY: Harper and Row, 1971), p. 39.
7 Andrew Whitaker, *Einstein, Bohr and the Quantum Dilemma* (Cambridge: Cambridge University Press, 1996), pp. 4–13; Robert Martin
   Eisberg, *Fundamentals of Modern Physics,* (New York: Wiley, 1961),
   pp. 108–109.

which reduce the atom to a mere arrangement of its parts, are insufficient to explain the observations and measurements of physicists. The parts cannot exist in complete actuality; they are dependent on the atom, which is a whole. This means that, at least in some cases, the whole cannot be explained by its parts and mechanistic explanations are insufficient.

These two arguments, one based on our own awareness and interiority, the other based on the explanation of the atom by modern science, give us good reason to conclude that we, and other material beings as well, have a greater unity than that of a machine; that in the case of natural substances, the whole is prior to the part. But, at the same time, arguing for the substantial oneness of complex beings such as dogs, seems to ignore something obvious: Our observations, which themselves have a beginning in experience, make it clear that living things are made up of and depend on carbon, iodine, calcium, and many other chemical elements. A deficiency of the chemical element iodine can cause headaches, poor memory, and depression. The effects of damaging the brain are even more dramatic. The operation of our senses and even of our minds depends on the condition of our organs and on the chemical elements which they contain. Merely asserting the unity of living thing seems to ignore or to willfully disregard the actual material nature of living things.

Inescapably, then, if the living thing is a single substance, it is a substance which depends in very important ways on its parts (as does an atom, for that matter). So, on the one hand, a living thing is really and substantially one and not reducible to its parts. It is not an aggregate, just a collection of iodine, carbon, and other chemicals. Yet, on the other hand, the living thing still contains and is still dependent on its parts. So if a living thing is just one substance, all dog, say, we still need to account for the presence of organs and elements in this dog.

In fact, the realization that living things are both substantially one and at the same time complex and (somehow) contain parts is not new. Aristotle and Thomas Aquinas address the question of the unity and complexity of living things, and their answer, referred to as virtual presence or presence by power, is a satisfactory solution. Aristotle proposes this solution in *On Generation and Corruption,* where he says, very concisely, that in complex bodies or, as he calls them, mixed bodies, the elements are present *by power.*[8]

At first, the statement that an element is present *by power* or *by its powers* seems rather cryptic. To make this formula clearer, we need to talk about what an element is and how an element relates to its powers. Aristotle, in the *Metaphysics,* defines an element as: "The first constituent of which a thing is composed and which is indivisible in kind into other kinds."[9] This definition has two parts. First, an element is something which is not completely destroyed in a complex substance. Rather, it somehow remains in the substance of which it is an element, as is obviously the case. Second, an element is not composed of anything more fundamental, so that it cannot be divided into parts that are themselves different in kind.

It is, of course, quite clear that none of the four things Aristotle identified as elements is truly elemental. But when we come to explain why none of his elements are truly elemental, we continue to use Aristotle's own definition of element. It is precisely because earth, air, fire, and water can be broken down into things that are different in kind that they are not really elements. And when the present-day chemical elements were named elements, it was because they were thought to fulfill Aristotle's definition as the most fundamental components of physical things. It is for the same reason that the most fundamental particles — which could possibly be the real elements — are called elementary. So, while we do not consider earth, air, fire, or water to be really elements, the ancient and modern use of the word "element" are the same: when we talk about elements today, we continue to use Aristotle's definition.[10]

8 Aristotle, *De Generatione et Corruptione,* ed. Harold H. Joachim (Oxford: Clarendon Press, 1922; reprint, Hildesheim: Georg Olms, 1970), bk. II, chap. 1–4, 7; See also St. Thomas Aquinas, *De Mixtione Elementorum,* ln. 123–153.
9 Aristotle, *Metaphysics,* trans. Hippocrates G. Apostle (Grinnell, Iowa: The Peripatetic Press, 1979), bk. V, 3, 1014a26–27.
10 *Ibid.*

(In my exposition of the thought of Aristotle and Thomas, however, I will speak in terms of the Empedoclean elements, earth, air, fire, and water. This will allow me to present the Thomistic understanding of the elements more accurately, but is not, of course, an assertion that these are actually elements.)

Aristotle and Thomas Aquinas understand the elements to be distinguished by their powers, by means of which they act on and react to the world: Fire is hot and dry, air hot and moist, water cool and moist, and earth cool and dry. Chemical elements and elementary particles are similarly specified by powers such as mass, electronegativity, charge, and spin. It is by means of these active and passive powers that the elements act on and are acted on by each other.[11]

So when Aristotle says that the elements are present *by their powers,* he means that the active and passive qualities of the elements are in some way preserved in the mixed body, while the elements themselves do not remain in a mixed body *as substances.* That is, the substantial forms of the elements do not, strictly speaking, continue to exist, but the powers of the elements remain in the mixed body. However, the active and passive powers of the elements are contraries. (For example, the heat of fire is contrary to the coldness of water.) Therefore, the qualities of all the elements involved cannot be actually present in the mixed body, since a mixed body composed of fire and water cannot be actually hot and cold at the same time. But, these qualities, unlike the substantial forms of the elements, can be possessed to a greater or lesser degree. Thus, in a mixed body "a mean quality which partakes [*sapiat:* savors] of the nature of each extreme"[12] can be brought about from the qualities of the elements. For example, grey is in some way like both black and white, and tepid like both hot and cold.[13]

---

11 Aristotle, *De Generatione et Corruptione.,* bk. II, 1–4, 7; Joseph Bobik, *Aquinas on Matter and Form and the Elements,* (Notre Dame, Ind.: University of Notre Dame Press, 1998), pp. 167–172.

12 Aquinas, *De Mixtione Elementorum,* ln. 125–128. The English translation is from Bobik, p. 121.

13 *Ibid.,* ln. 123–132; Christopher A. Decaen, "Elemental Virtual Presence in St. Thomas," *The Thomist* 64 (2000): pp. 287–294.

In the mixed body, this intermediate quality is that mixed body's proper quality, just as the unaltered qualities of the elements are the proper qualities of the elements. For example, heat and dryness are the proper qualities of fire, while a certain degree of tepidness and humidity would be the proper quality of a mixed body composed of fire and water. The qualities of the elements are found in this middle quality of the mixed body in the same way that extremes "are found in a mean which shares [*participat*] the nature of each of them."[14] So the proper qualities of the elements cannot be said to be actually preserved—the full heat of fire is not found in a mixed body of which it is an element—but the powers of the elements are found in the power of the mixed body partially, because the mean shares in, participates, possesses in part, the extremes.[15]

Of course, in living things there are cells, tissues, and organs, each of which is an additional layer of complexity between the most elemental particles and the living organism. As I argued above, the unity of a living thing is a fundamental fact of our experience, a starting point rather than a conclusion. Because of this, all the parts of a living thing, ranging from atoms and cells to heart and brain, cannot be present as substances; they must depend on the whole living thing. And since they cannot be substances, being present as a part can only mean being present as shape, color, texture, etc., in some quantitative part, dependent on the substantial form of the whole.[16]

It might seem strange to say that a part such as an eye, that you can see and touch, is present in a way analogous to the way an element is present. That is, to say that an eye just is certain powers in a certain quantitative part of the body seems rather odd. But we know that iron is localized in hemoglobin just because of the accidents of iron present in that part of the blood, and we know that we have an eye just because we have a sensation of certain sensible qualities

14 Aquinas, *De Mixtione Elementorum*, ln. 137–140.
15 *Ibid.*, 123–140; Decaen, "Elemental Virtual Presence," pp. 287–294.
16 Michael Storck "*Pars Integralis* in St. Thomas Aquinas and the Parts of Living Substances," *The Thomist* 78 (2014), pp. 379–399.

in a certain part of the body. And if a thing has either an accidental or a substantial form, and a part of a substance cannot have a substantial form, then a part must be certain specific accidents of the human substance in a certain (quantitative) part of the substance, just as an element is present in a living thing as certain specific powers.[17]

So far, my argument has been based in great part on our awareness of our own unity. Plants, however, seem — although claims to the contrary have been made — to lack the inside view which we so clearly have, and which we are fairly certain that the animals of which we have the most experience (dogs, for example) also have. This internal view is one of our strongest arguments for the unity of animals. In the case of plants, then, what sort of argument can we make that they are really one thing?

When Thomas discusses living things, he says that the activities of a plant (unlike those of an animal) are carried out by means of the powers of corporeal nature. That is, to describe a cell dividing in terms of its organelles does not miss the point in the same way that describing an act of seeing in terms of neurons firing does. Yet, while the activities of a plant are carried out by the powers of corporeal nature, a plant's activities differ from those of non-living things because they come from an internal principle.[18]

As a result, whether or not a living thing is *formed* by chance, it still must *be* more than simply a collection of parts that just happens to act in a regular way. It is analogous to hydrogen and oxygen just happening to come together under conditions that cause them to unite and become water. In such a case, the water acts like water not by chance, but because it is a certain kind of thing, because it has the nature of water. Similarly, even if the necessary elements just happen to come together in just the right way to form a bacterium

17 But see Aquinas, *Summa Theologiae*, 1, q. 75, a. 2, ad 1; 1, q. 29, a. 1, ad 2; 1 q. 76, a. 5, ad 3; and 3 q. 90, a. 3; idem, *Commentaria in Octo Libros Physicorum Aristotelis*, 1.9. 8–9; and idem, *Quaestiones disputatae de anima*, q. 9.
18 Aquinas, *Summa Theologiae*, I, q. 78, a. 1–2; and *In De Anima* 1, lec. 14, ln. 10–21, 2, lec. 7, ln. 47–60.

or a tree, it is not by chance that the tree or the bacterium acts and lives in a tree-like or bacterium-like way.[19]

Further, if an oak tree were only a chance collection of parts that happened to work together to produce certain activities, then it would not be reasonable to expect the same effect to result always or for the most part from such a random collection of parts. But an oak tree does always produce a certain kind of nut, and leaves of a certain size and pattern, because it is a particular kind of thing, even if that thing happens to have been produced by chance. The oak's life has a stability that follows from its nature as just this kind of thing in the same way that water's properties follow from its nature as this specific kind of thing, so that chance has brought about, not a chance assemblage, but a thing, a substance of a certain kind: a particular oak. And, even though a self-reproducing machine might not be in principle impossible, still, such a machine would not reproduce as does a living thing, because it does not exist in the way a plant does. It does not live. If we imagine such a machine, we see it taking in material from its environment and shaping it into new machines. This is not like the reproduction of a living thing. A single-celled living thing, and each of the cells composing a multi-cellular living thing, divides itself into two similar parts (based on, as Thomas says, its internal principle). In the living thing, there is not the same distinction between a part that acts and another part that is acted on (as we would imagine there would be in the self-replicating machine). Rather, reproduction is something that the living thing as a whole does. Sexual reproduction differs even more from the machine's self-duplication. Here, each parent contributes a cell having half the genetic material for the offspring, and these cells unite to form a new cell which, while resembling the adult organism only genetically, is able to grow and develop into an adult of the same species.[20]

19   Aristotle, *Physics*, bk. II, 8.
20   *Richard Connell, Substance and Modern Science (Houston: Center for Thomistic Studies, 1988),* pp. 110–117; Hans Jonas, *The Phenomenon of Life: Toward a Philosophical Biology* (New York: Harper and Row, 1966; reprint, Evanston, Ill.: Northwestern University Press, 2001), pp. 76n, 99–106.

The vegetative powers (common to plants and animals) include not only reproduction, but also growth and development, nutrition, homeostasis and metabolism. All these powers perform their activities, as Thomas says, by means of the powers of the elements, but the activities exceed the power of non-living things because they proceed from within, from an intrinsic principle. For example, reproduction is carried out by the powers of carbon, DNA, RNA, etc., but by the powers of these things as parts of the living organism. So while the unity of an animal, and most especially our own unity, is definitely more certain and more obvious than that of a plant, plants too exhibit a unity not found in a machine or an aggregate. It follows that, just as in the case of an animal, the parts of a plant — not only the most fundamental parts, but also more fundamental yet still not truly elemental parts like cells and tissues — are best understood as present by their powers in quantitative parts of the plant.[21]

And, as Hans Jonas points out, the very existence of a living thing requires it to have a relationship and connection with the world around it in a way that is deeper than and different from anything in the non-living world. A machine can exist indefinitely on a shelf (as long as it is properly rust-proofed). A living plant without water, soil, nutrients, and sunlight will die. While the existence of a rock or machine does not essentially depend on its surroundings, even the simplest living thing can no longer exist as living without a certain environment and a specific sort of relationship with that environment.[22]

Ultimately, the question whether something is a substance or an aggregate is not one that can be directly answered by measurement or experiment. Substantial forms exceed the grasp of the senses, and, to the extent that experimental science restricts itself to what can be measured and sensed, substantial forms exceed the grasp of experimental science. After all, we never directly sense or measure the nature of anything. Everything we directly sense and measure, size, color, mass,

---

21 Aquinas, *Summa Theologiae*, I, q. 78, a. 1.
22 *Ibid.*; See also, Jonas, *The Phenomenon of Life*, pp. 84–86.

spin, charge or temperature, is an accident. We know that the human body contains carbon, not because we observe the nature of a carbon atom in the human body, but because we observe the accidents, the powers, of a carbon atom. The reason that carbon is essential to all life (at least within our experience) is its property of being able to form very large molecules, including amino acids (which compose proteins), lipids (which compose many of a living thing's membranes, including cell walls in animals), and DNA molecules. Without this unique property of carbon, life as we know it could not exist. And presence by power, as understood by Thomas, explains how this complexity exists within the substantial unity of the living thing. It explains how the powers of carbon and the other elements, all the material parts which make up our bodies, all the things which our senses tell us about the complexity of living things, and everything measurable and explainable by experimental science, can exist in a substantial whole.[23]

St. Thomas's account of presence by power, then, explains the role of the elements as parts of complex bodies, and at the same time allows mixed bodies and living things to be real substantial unities. This same presence by power is not refuted by the discoveries of modern physics, and can even help us understand what physics is saying about the relation between parts and wholes at an atomic level. Furthermore, because presence by power is more general than the primarily microscopic domain of quantum theory, it allows us to understand the existence of parts in wholes in a more universal way which includes living things.

23 Aquinas, *Summa Theologiae*, I-II, q. 31, a. 5; See also, James Jeans, *The Mysterious Universe* (New York: Macmillan, 1930), pp. 9–11.

3

Hierarchy in a New Natural Science

> The hierarchy of creatures is expressed by the order of the "six days," from the less perfect to the more perfect. God loves all his creatures and takes care of each one, even the sparrow. Nevertheless, Jesus said: "You are of more value than many sparrows," or again: "Of how much more value is a man than a sheep!"[1]

MODERN SECULAR MAN DISAGREES that man is more valuable than a sparrow or a sheep. No being in this universe has more value than any other being; indeed, no being has any intrinsic value at all. All value judgments are imposed arbitrarily by human will. Nature is seen, as Pope Francis says, as "something form-less, completely open to manipulation."[2] It is investigated in order to be used. The universe is a meaningless assemblage of bodies moving according to natural laws, from which life and man emerged by chance. We came to be for no reason and have no reason to live for any particular goal. This dreary prospect lends itself to hedonism or epicureanism for the more sophisticated. Seek pleasure or tranquility. Distract yourself from despair.

The Church has always taught the opposite, as reiterated by Pope Francis in *Laudato si'*, "Each creature possesses its own particular goodness and perfection... Each of the various creatures, willed in its own being, reflects in its own way a ray of God's infinite wisdom and goodness. Man must therefore respect the particular goodness of every creature, to avoid any disordered use of things."[3] A truer more adequate

---

1 *Catechism of the Catholic Church*, no. 2416.
2 Pope Francis, *Laudato si'*, no. 106.
3 *Catechism of the Catholic Church*, 339. Cited by Pope Francis, *Laudato si',* no. 69.

investigation of Nature reveals that creatures do indeed have intrinsic goodness and vary radically in their worth. Scientists that approach the world with openness to a hierarchy in nature are able to discover a host of meanings hidden from a value-free utilitarian approach to nature. In this chapter I will highlight the vast differences in the grades of being in nature and reflect on how grasping a hierarchy in nature can enrich the way we study nature. I will describe two research areas in biology that take their point of departure from the difference among the grades of animals.

A NEW NATURAL SCIENCE

In *the Abolition of Man*, C. S. Lewis calls for "a new Natural Philosophy." He compares the goal of the science of earlier ages "to conform the soul to reality"[4] to the present goal of contemporary science "to subdue reality to the wishes of men."[5]

> Is it then possible to imagine a new Natural Philosophy, continually conscious that the 'natural object' produced by analysis and abstraction is not reality, but only a view, and always correcting the abstraction? I hardly know what I am asking for. I hear rumors that Goethe's approach to nature deserves fuller consideration . . . The regenerate science which I have in mind would not do even to minerals and vegetables what modern science threatens to do to man himself. When it explained it would not explain away. When it spoke of the parts, it would remember the whole.[6]

Francis Bacon and Descartes set out modernity's program of pursuing knowledge useful to man and its success has been prodigious. There is no doubt that science has given men (at least some men) more control over nature and safer, more comfortable lives, although there is also a dark side to this increase of useful knowledge. Understanding the atom has given us bombs as well as power plants. Factories pollute the

4 C. S. Lewis, *The Abolition of Man* (New York: HarperCollins Publishers, 1974), p. 77.
5 *Ibid.*, p. 77.
6 *Ibid.*, p. 79.

air and water and lay waste the landscape even as they churn out more consumer goods to make our lives more comfortable or entertaining. Yet almost no one wants to stop the pursuit of knowledge. Nor can most people imagine a different sort of natural science. What other way is there to study nature than by the scientific method?

Unfortunately, the modern world view only asks certain questions and so it is only likely to discover certain answers. Most scientists work within a materialistic framework that regards questions about goodness, beauty, and meaning as nonsensical. C. S. Lewis compares our Model of the Universe to a stencil. "It determines how much of that total truth will appear and what pattern it will suggest."[7] Even scientists who would like to think outside the box are forced to conform to the system. They will not get research grants, nor have their articles published, nor get tenure or promotions if they stray.

> Science is not simply the answering of questions; it is also the choosing of which questions to ask.... Facts and data do not just present themselves to us. Experimental and observational studies must be formulated and conducted, often at great cost.... This is commonly done in the service of one or more research programs.... But these programs grow out of an extended dialogue within a community of scientists, or due to funding pressures, and either way are the product of the norms, values, and interests of broader society. Thus these norms and values shape not only what qualifies as evidence, but what evidence is even available to be considered in need of explanation.[8]

What appears through the scientific establishment stencil and how might we access what is hidden? The stencil allows scientists to pursue questions about what things are made of, especially their smallest parts, how they are put together

7   C. S. Lewis, *The Discarded Image* (Cambridge: Cambridge University Press, 2013), p. 223.
8   William A. Wilson, "The Myth of Scientific Objectivity," *First Things*, November 2017. Online at https://www.firstthings.com/article/2017/11/the-myth-of-scientific-objectivity Accessed July 24, 2020.

and how some things move other things. What is left out? The whole world of lived experience: all the colors, smells, tastes and sounds, pleasures and pains of the real world. Life, consciousness, goodness and beauty are considered "subjective" and illusory. Scientists are encouraged, or forced by career considerations, to research and publish about aspects of the world that can be described in quantitative relationships. Graphs are good; equations are better. Narrowing in on biology, few can publish anything that casts doubt on a purely mechanistic version of Neo-Darwinism. No natures, in the sense of essence, and no teleology can be part of an *orthodox* interpretation of research.

However, not all scientists since Bacon and Descartes have been mechanists; there has been a slender stream of unorthodox biologists who have kept their focus on the whole organism and its form and activities.[9] Many of them in the last century trace a connection to Goethe, the great Romantic poet and natural philosopher, whom C. S. Lewis mentions. Goethe was a master of reading the *Gestalt* or form of organisms. He understood the *Gestalt* as the "living idea" of the plant or animal which unites the parts of the outer structure into a whole.[10] Goethe was a strong influence on Adolf Portmann, a Swiss zoologist who did brilliant work on the meaning of animal appearances, activities, and social life. Portmann's work can give us an idea of what a new natural science could be like. He observes nature with openness to the phenomena, unafraid to observe things that do not fit a mechanistic Darwinian model.

HIERARCHY: A FORBIDDEN TOPIC

One of the forbidden topics in modern science is hierarchy among organisms (i.e., that some kinds of living things are

9 In *Approaches to a Philosophical Biology* (New York: Basic Books, 1968), Marjorie Greene reviews the work of several Europeans interested in a holistic approach to biology including Adolf Portmann, Helmuth Plessner, F. J. J. Buytendijk, Erwin Strauss, and Kurt Goldstein. Both Hans Jonas and Leon Kass also pursued such an approach in the United States. See footnotes nos. 15, 16, and 18.

10 Johann Wolfgang von Goethe, "On Morphology" in *Goethe Scientific Studies,* ed. and trans. Douglas Miller (New York: Suhrkamp Publishers, 1988), pp. 63–64.

more perfect than others). Most scientists who ascribe to Neo-Darwinism explicitly reject it. They believe that ultimate particles are the real beings; everything else is an epiphenomenon of the arrangement and motion of ultimate particles. Animals and plants are more or less complicated bundles of chemical reactions. As Nobel Prize-winner, Jacques Monod writes succinctly, "Living beings are chemical machines."[11] There is only a quantitative difference between living and non-living. "Living beings may be distinguished from all other beings including crystals by a purely quantitative criterion. They can transmit a quantity of information several orders of magnitude greater than any non-living being."[12]

Neo-Darwinism excludes any basis for counting one organism higher than another since all natural beings are conglomerations of molecules, products of blind chance. If all that is important is a superior power of survival and reproduction, then bacteria are better adapted than humans.

> The chimpanzee and the human share about 99.5 per cent of their evolutionary history, yet most human thinkers regard themselves as stepping-stones to the Almighty. To an evolutionist this cannot be so. There exists no objective basis on which to elevate one species above another. Chimp and human, lizard and fungus, we have all evolved over some three billion years by a process known as natural selection.[13]

Neo-Darwinists hold not only that there are no essential differences between different kinds of natural beings like lizards and humans; but also, that there are no true species. There are only individuals that are more or less like each other. While common sense and Catholic doctrine suggest that that this is nonsense, mechanism has obscured for many the significance of hierarchy in nature.

11 Jacques Monod, *Chance and Necessity: An Essay on the Natural Philosophy of Modern Biology* (New York: Vintage Books, 1971), p. 45.
12 *Ibid.*, p. 13.
13 Robert Trivers, Forward to *The Selfish Gene*, by Richard Dawkins (New York: Oxford University Press, 1976), p. *v*.

OBSERVING HIERARCHY

The best way to investigate hierarchy in nature is to look at the differences in the qualities and activities of members of distinct grades of beings. Let us look at the differences: *first* between living and nonliving creatures; *second*, between plants and animals; *third*, between different levels of animals; and *fourth*, between irrational animals and men.

LIVING AND NON-LIVING

When one looks at living things such as oak trees or elephants and compares them to nonliving things such as rocks or lakes, one is struck by their unity and goodness. They can do many more things. Chip away at a rock and it will get smaller but not less rock. It does not seem to *do* anything to stop one from chipping away at it. It is indifferent. But living things are in no way indifferent. They constantly do things *for themselves*. As soon as there is life, there is inclination, because living things must constantly metabolize, take in nourishment to maintain themselves or they die.[14] Darwinian theory takes as a given the "struggle for existence," that all living things try as hard as they can to preserve their life and reproduce.

In generation an acorn *develops itself* in an orderly way from a simple seed into an enormous oak tree. Likewise, an elephant develops itself from a single-celled zygote into a two-ton mature elephant, like its parents. This development does not just consist of adding more molecules like more Lego bricks to make a bigger Lego elephant. Living things *organize themselves* and build themselves different kinds of parts[15]. They are immensely complex wholes consisting of trillions of parts ordered in levels from molecules to cells, to tissues, to organs, to systems, to the whole. At every level each part has a specific function, which serves the whole. Living things also *maintain themselves*. They take in nourishment and turn it into themselves or into fuel for their activities or

---

14 Hans Jonas, *The Phenomenon of Life*: *Toward a More Philosophical Biology*, (Harper and Row, 1066; Chicago: University of Chicago Press, 1982) p. 4.
15 Leon R. Kass, M. D., *Toward a More Natural Science*, (New York: The Free Press, 1985), pp. 254–257.

warmth. Living things *heal themselves.* If they are cut, they regrow tissue. Plant cuttings often grow into a whole plant. Many animals have immune systems, which protect the animal from infections.

Ordinary experience tells us that living things *act for a purpose.* Life is good and living things work to maintain their life and to pass it on to their offspring. They grow, develop, and organize themselves toward a goal, the mature form of the organism. They nourish themselves and heal themselves for a goal, to preserve their lives. They spin webs, build nests, and burrow tunnels for a variety of goals. The many activities that animals perform in order to maintain and reproduce their life become part of their purpose. It is good to be a bird and this goodness includes eating juicy worms, flying, singing and building nests. Even plants exhibit purposeful activities besides generation and development, such as bending towards the light. These activities are not consciously directed by the organism the way a man weaves a blanket or builds a house; nevertheless, the organism clearly works for many goals that are good for it or its species.[16]

Thus, we see many differences between living and non-living things. An organism is an individual, which moves itself toward inwardly determined goals. It acts for its own sake. It develops itself, organizes itself, maintains itself, and reproduces itself. Life "exhibits in each individual instance a striving of its own for existence and fulfillment."[17] Organisms are not only more complex structures than non-living beings; they also have the capacities for many more kinds of activities. They have a richer way of being.

PLANTS

Next, let us consider the life of a plant. Since it is without mobility, a plant must be contiguous with its food source. It must continually metabolize and so it must continually take in nourishment. It takes in what is other to change it

16 Leon R. Kass, M. D., "The Permanent Limitations of Biology," *The Ambiguous Legacy of the Enlightenment,* ed. William A. Rusher (Lanham, Maryland: University Press of America, 1995), pp. 120–141.
17 Jonas, *Phenomenon of Life,* p. 61.

into itself. There is a very limited relation between the plant and other things; the plant's need corresponds to its inclination to keep bringing in food and metabolizing it. The plant stays rooted in the ground as it develops into its mature form and reproduces it. It achieves its highpoint in flowering and bearing fruit. It produces and reproduces a magnificent form.[18] The plant reaches beyond itself by displaying itself and by reproduction. By its reproductive power the plant reaches beyond the individual to its offspring. In this way it approaches the sensitive power of animals, which can reach out to all bodies.[19]

ANIMALS

The simplest animal has a higher power than plants. It transcends its matter by sensation. It takes in the form of the other *as other*, not in order to consume it, but to know it. Sensation always involves an elementary form of consciousness; which plants lack altogether. With knowledge comes appetite. Following the sensation of objects, there follows a conscious attitude toward the object sensed, either desire or fear. Hence, the animal stands as a self, vis-à-vis the world, unlike a plant. It stands at a distance and perceives and moves towards what it desires or flees what it fears. Thus, the three powers of sensation, appetite, and local motion are connected to each other and the distance the animal has from its food.[20] But they are not restricted to helping the animal obtain food; they also make possible communication, social life with courting and parenting, making things like nests or tunnels, and even play.

Sensation has many grades of perfection in animals. It can vary from the primitive feeling of pain that causes an amoeba to flee certain chemical substances to a musician listening to a Beethoven symphony. At the lowest end, sensation is difficult to distinguish from plant tropisms. There is, however, a clear distinction between sensations in higher animals like lions and tropisms in higher plants like sunflowers. The lion sees

---

18 *Ibid.*, pp. 99–107.
19 *Summa Theologiae*, I, q. 78, a. 2.
20 Jonas, *Phenomenon*, pp. 104–105 and Aristotle, *De anima*, bk. III, 9–10, 432a–433b.

a gazelle and desires to devour it, so he dashes after it. The sunflower, on the other hand, bends toward the sun without possessing any awareness of it. In phototropism, sunlight destroys plant growth hormones on the sunny side of the plant. This causes the cells in the shaded side of the plant to grow longer. The longer cells on the shaded side cause the stem to bend toward the light.

GRADES OF ANIMALS

Recent studies of animal behavior and instincts have been a counterweight to the excessive focus on biological parts in biochemistry and molecular genetics. Ethologists have found that instincts, innate inherited behaviors of animals, are more variegated than expected. Some behaviors are inherited in a rigid form, while other behaviors are more flexible and open to change. Bird song is a lovely example. Some birds such as warblers, even if raised in complete isolation, will begin to sing the typical song of their species as soon as they are old enough. Other birds, such as finches, need to learn their species' song. If they only hear the song of another species during their youth, they will learn the song of the other species and sing it the rest of their life. A third group of birds, however, such as mockingbirds or parrots, retain openness to learning new songs or sounds, during their whole life.[21]

We will sketch a few representative behaviors in animals of different rank in order to see what light animal behavior sheds on hierarchy. If animals reach their fulfillment in their activities, we should find in their activities a "progressively richer realization of the idea, the type of animal life."[22]

SPONGES: PORIFERA

First, we will look at some of the lowest invertebrates, sponges. They can barely be distinguished from plants. They always live attached to rocks in the sea. Their life consists in

21 Adolf Portmann, "The Special Position of Man in the Realm of the Living," trans. Werner J. Dannhauser, *Commentary* (November 1965), pp. 39–40.
22 F. J. J. Buytendijk cited in *Approaches to a Philosophical Biology,* ed. Marjorie Greene (New York: Basic Books, 1968), p. 147.

siphoning seawater; they take in seawater, digest the micro-organisms floating in it and then expel it. Their only sense is touch, but since they have no central nervous system only the cells that are actually touched respond to stimuli. They live next to each other but have no social life.[23]

HUNTING WASPS

Insects already show a much higher degree of awareness and behavior. Let us look at some experiments of Henri Fabre with digger-wasps. The mother wasp of each species preys on only one particular quarry: one species of locust, spider, beetle or caterpillar. The female *Ammophila carpentris* immobilizes a large caterpillar with eight stings each in exactly the right place along the back to paralyze but not kill it.[24] Then she drags the prey into the hole she has dug and lays an egg on it. When the larva hatches, it finds fresh meat waiting for it. She is clearly no machine; she must find and recognize the hawk-moth caterpil-lar; she must find the exact spots to sting her prey; she must remember where her hole is and drag the prey down into it. There is a remarkable wisdom to her instinct but also remark-able limitations. When Fabre removed the caterpillar and egg from the breeding hole, she carefully closed it up in the same way as if there were still an egg to protect; she was unable to change her behavior when the reason for it disappeared.[25]

BIRDS

Birds exhibit a much richer way of life. They care for their eggs in the nest by sitting on them; they feed their voracious progeny after hatching; and they teach them how to fly, how to scratch for bugs, how to sing their species' song, and even what to fear.[26] Many bird "couples" cooperate in incubating

23 Lynn Margulis and Karlene V. Schwarz, *Five Kingdoms: An Illustrated Guide to the Phyla of Life on Earth* (New York: W. H. Freeman and Company, 1995), pp. 176–177.

24   J. Henri Fabre, *The Insect World of J. Henri Fabre*, ed. Edwin Way Teale and trans. Alexander Teixeira de Mattos (Boston: Beacon Press, 1991), pp. 388–389.

25 *Ibid.*, pp. 197–202.

26 Konrad Z. Lorenz, *King Solomon's Ring: New Light on Animal Ways* (New York: Meridian Books, 1952,) pp. 143–192.

the eggs and feeding the fledglings.[27] Most birds are monogamous, at least for the breeding season, and many for years, or even a lifetime, as banding birds is demonstrating. This is especially astonishing in the case of migratory birds, which may fly thousands or even tens of thousands of kilometers twice a year on their migratory journeys. Monogamous birds clearly recognize and are attached to their mate.[28]

MAMMALS

We have most familiarity with mammals. They live with us as pets or farm animals and we observe them sensing and feeling emotions. They communicate with us by their barks and wagging tails. Nobel prize-winning naturalist Konrad Lorenz describes canine communication in the following passage.

> When your dog nuzzles you, whines, runs to the door and scratches it, or puts his paws on the wash basin under the tap, and looks at you imploringly, he does something that comes far nearer to human speech than anything that a jackdaw or goose can ever "say," ... The dog wants to make you open the door or turn on the tap, and what he does has the specific and purposeful motive of influencing you in a certain direction.[29]

These behaviors of dogs are not innate. Each dog learns how to make its needs known to its owner in its own way and can adapt its methods of communication to the situation.

Higher mammals possess an amazing ability to learn, which is sometimes mistaken for rationality. Chimpanzees can solve problems like how to get bananas that are too high to reach; they can make tools by plucking twigs, pulling off the leaves and sticking them into termite holes to fish out termites. They can also be taught to use sign language or plastic chips to indicate things they want.[30]

27 Adolf Portmann, *Animal Forms and Patterns: A Study of the Appearance of Animals* (New York: Schocken Books, 1967), pp. 151–164.
28 Adolf Portmann, *Animals as Social Beings* (New York: The Viking Press, 1961), 219–233.
29 Lorenz, *King Solomon's Ring*, pp. 99–100.
30 Marie George, "Thomas Aquinas Meets Nim Chimpsky: On the

Mammals also have a large capacity for affection. Max, a friend's horse, moped so disconsolately when his owner went off to college that a donkey was bought to keep him company. He soon cheered up and became good "friends" with the donkey. They were inseparable companions for years until Max died at a ripe old age. Many dogs are strongly attached to their masters. Dogs like to sleep near their master's chair; a walk is a hundred times more enjoyable when their master accompanies them.

In the wild, many kinds of mammals like wolves, elephants, and primates have elaborate social behaviors connected with hunting, courting, mating, childcare and social ranking. They live in packs with rulers and work together to get food and protect the pack.

Thus, there are clearly different grades of animals from sponges to primates. As one considers animals in ascending grades, they show themselves to possess more and more clearly their own center of consciousness, emotion, and action. They demonstrate an increasing ability to learn, to communicate with others, to interact socially, and to show affection.

MAN: ANIMAL WITH A DIFFERENCE

Yet, there is still a higher way of being alive, our own human way. We can think and talk; we can perform experiments, write books, paint, sing, build cities and cathedrals and worship God in them. We know that we are decisively different from other animals by the very fact that we are the only ones that can wonder about the difference. It is the powers of reason and will that make man essentially different. Our unique way of experiencing the world and acting on it as well as our ways of communicating with each other and living together are the more remarkable because we are so similar to our nearest animal cousins, the primates, in our sense organs, brains, and whole bodily structure. Yet what could be more different from a formal dinner party than an ape gulping down a banana? In the one case there is feeding,

Debate about Human Nature and the Nature of Other Animals," *The Aquinas Review* 10 (2003): pp. 1–50.

satisfaction of a primary appetite, in the other case there is dining, in which the food takes secondary place to the social communications for which it provides the opportunity.[31]

There is a radical discontinuity between man and beast, even the highest primates. Thinking is essentially different from sensing. It involves grasping the universal natures of things, while sensing is awareness of particular sensible bodies. Since man can grasp universal natures, he can use language. He gives names to the natures that he understands. Members of a culture can communicate with each other because they have established by convention the names to be used as symbols for these natures. Hence language is rightly considered a sign of rationality. Moreover, through reason man can think about all of being. He can acquire science because he can understand the natures and properties of things. Thus, science is also a sign of rationality. Furthermore, through reason, man can grasp (in a partial way) the natures of immaterial things; hence belief in God or gods and the immortality of the soul and in general religion is a most certain sign of rationality.

Through reason, man also has an essentially new level of freedom. Because he has an intellect, which is capable of grasping universal being and a will capable of loving universal goodness, he can understand his natural ends as ends and choose suitable means to achieve them. He can understand and compare various natural ends like nutrition and religion and choose to fast from food as an act of worship. The ends he shares with animals like nourishment or reproduction are fulfilled in a new human context. Fulfilling the demands of friendship (as in marriage), the intellectual life (as in Plato's *Symposium*) or religious life (as in sacred meals like the Passover or the Mass) regulate and enrich the animal acts of eating or generation to an essentially new level. The ability to set goals, especially immaterial goals, and to devise the means to acquire them is a sign of man's rationality.

Paradoxically, human freedom is perfected most of all in a voluntary bond, a vow. Both in marriage and in the religious

31   Leon R. Kass, M. D., *The Hungry Soul: Eating and the Perfection of Our Nature* (Chicago: The University of Chicago Press, 1999), pp. 131–192.

life, humans hold the rest of their life in their hands and promise to live by a certain form until death. They give themselves in their entirety either to a human spouse in marriage or to their divine spouse in the religious life. In this gift-of-self "the whole person including the temporal dimension is present."[32] This gift-of-self is possible only for humans, because they are the only animals that possess themselves in their reflective self-consciousness and freedom.

Clearly there is an order from less perfect to more perfect beings in nature. As one considers the difference between nonliving and living beings, between plants and lower animals; between lower animals and higher animals; and between animals and man, one sees more unity, more capacities for operations, more knowledge, more freedom, and more love. There is a greater inwardness and a progressively richer way of being.

HIERARCHY AND THE STUDY OF NATURE

Recognizing a hierarchy in nature opens up many questions that would never occur to a scientist who is a mechanist. We will look at two of the many *unorthodox* questions which Adolf Portmann pursues. First, Adolf Portmann looks at animal appearances and asks what they mean. Second, he wonders why humans are born a year too early, still in an embryonic state at birth.

HIERARCHY AND THE APPEARANCE OF ANIMALS

The neo-Darwinian paradigm does not permit one to find any meaning in living things other than adaptation and survival. The beauty and striking appearances of organisms are such an obvious difficulty that Darwin said he would have to give up his theory of natural selection if it could ever be proved that beauty was a purpose in nature.[33] He developed an elaborate theory of sexual selection to explain why certain

---

32   John Paul II, *Familiaris Consortio*, (1981), no. 11.

33   "They believe that very many structures have been created for beauty in the eyes of man, or for mere variety. This doctrine, if true, would be absolutely fatal to my theory." Charles Darwin, *On the Origin of Species by Natural Selection*, Second Edition (New York: D. Appleton and Company, 1860), pp. 177–178.

animals have such colorful feathers or fanciful features. Since Adolf Portmann was free from the Darwinian straitjacket, he could admit what he observed: First, many animals appear to be designed to be beautiful or impressive in appearance and, second, some kinds of animals are more intelligent and have a richer way of living than others. Portmann decided to investigate whether there is a correspondence between appearance and rank in the hierarchy. He spent years on this investigation with all the resources of a modern scientific laboratory.

Portmann's first observation is that lower animals have no head. No unicellular animal, sponge, starfish, or jellyfish has a head. Many of the invertebrate phyla have no heads, whereas all of the vertebrates have heads. To have a head at all is already a characteristic of higher animals. It requires the concentration of the higher sense organs, the brain, and the mouth all at one pole of the body. It is the outward sign of a unified inner center of life, which controls nutrition, sensation, and locomotion. As one proceeds from lower ranked animals to higher, the head becomes more distinct. Fishes have a smooth streamlined form of body, which includes the head. Birds and mammals have more distinct heads. But even among them, one finds a similar distinction between the forms of lower and higher ranked birds or mammals. Mammals of the lowest intelligence also show a streamlined form of body. The heads of moles and mice simply fit into the smooth form of the whole body. As one proceeds to animals of a higher rank, the head becomes more and more set off from the body. Higher animals have a neck, which lifts the head above the line of the body. Chinese water deer and giraffes are closely related, but how different in form! The long neck and legs of the giraffe point to its much higher rank.[34]

Higher animals also have special formations of hair such as manes, whiskers or beards, which help separate the head from the rest of the body. Special colors and patterns also accentuate the head. Lower animals usually have a uniform color or pattern spread over the whole body, which does not emphasize the head. A good example is chipmunks whose

34 Portmann, *Animal Forms*, pp. 68–86.

stripes run from the tail to the inconspicuously colored head. The patterns on higher mammals are strikingly different; they emphasize the head as do horns, antlers and tusks. The big horn mountain goat's white neck and huge white curved horns set off the dark face dramatically.

There is often a similar difference between the patterns in the juvenile and mature forms of an animal as that between low and high-ranking animals. A wild bush piglet has stripes which end before the dull brown head while the adult bush pig has a beige body with an impressive head. It has a black eye area framed by white rims around the eyes and large ears with long tufts of hair. The head is eye-catching. Birds also often have an inconspicuous grey or brown plumage in youth, followed by vivid colors or crests in the adult accentuating the head. Cardinals are a good example. Juveniles are grey, while the mature males are bright red with a showy crest on the head. Female birds often have inconspicuous plumage compared to the males, but brighter than the juveniles. Portmann suggests that these differences point to the youth's humbler place in the species.[35]

Portmann concludes that the outer appearances of animals are designed in such a way as to impress the eye of the beholder. They are visual organs designed for visual receivers. The animals' forms and color patterns have a presentation value which carries many meanings such as rank of species, maturity, and sex.[36] He could never have discovered these meanings had he not been open to the possibility of purpose in nature.

HUMANS' SECOND YEAR IN THE WOMB

Another question Portmann pursues is why human babies are born a year too early compared to other highly intelligent mammals like chimpanzees. Humans are born helpless like mice, but with wide-open eyes and ears ready to learn more in their first year of life than ever again. The human infant's bodily proportions and tremendous rate of growth

35 *Ibid.*, pp. 143–164.
36 *Ibid.*, p. 25.

are embryonic; their brains still need to increase four times their size at birth. At a year, human infants correspond to the stage of development of higher mammals like foals and monkeys at birth. Mechanist biologists explain human's premature birth by saying that the human skull is so big and the woman's pelvis so small that humans need to be born before they reach the stage of development of other primates at birth. While this may be a factor, other ways of solving this problem can be imagined such as selection for females with wider pelvises or even greater postpartum growth of skull and brain. Portmann suggests that humans' second period of embryonic growth needs to take place in the "social uterus" of the family because of humans' special openness to the world. Humans need more than nourishment and the security of their mother's body to develop normally as humans. Their mind requires more sensible stimulation; their need for loving friendship must be fed and formed through the mother-child bond; their thinking needs the help of the family to teach them language. Even the purely physical characteristic of upright posture will not develop without the encouragement of the family.[37]

Portmann is able to grasp the meaning of human embryonic status at birth because he understands the essential difference of humans from other primates. Humans' unique openness to the world comes from their rationality, which sets them apart and above all other animals. Reason gives humans the need for a different infancy and childhood. The large size of the human skull also makes a premature birth necessary, but this too is connected to man's rationality for the larger brain is needed as an instrument for reason. The physiological needs correspond to the spiritual needs. Portmann's reflection on the need for the companionship of the family to achieve thought, language, relationships and even upright posture is most illuminating.

Similarly, Portmann is able to discover a meaning to animal appearances because he allows himself to contemplate the mysterious depth and beauty in the appearances of animals. He sees both that animal bodies are far more than physiological

37 Portmann, *Special Position,* pp. 38–41.

sacks for organs and that there are essential differences of rank among animal species. Therefore, he can wonder if there is any correlation between animal appearances and rank.

Adolf Portmann gives us a glimpse of a new natural science, the sort that C. S. Lewis wished for. When it explains, it does not explain away. When it speaks of the parts, it remembers the whole.[38] By taking off the blinders of materialist reductionism, scientists can grasp the grades of being in nature. This can suggest new paths to follow in investigating nature, paths that show meaning in many unexpected places.

38 C. S. Lewis, *The Abolition of Man* (New York: HarperCollins Publishers, 1974), p. 79.

4

Nature and Culture in Catholic Enviromentalism

ROMANO GUARDINI'S
LETTERS FROM LAKE COMO

CHRISTOPHER SHANNON

D OES CATHOLICISM HAVE ANYTHING distinct to contribute to the contemporary concern for restoring harmony in man's relation to nature? A brief consideration of the work of the theologian Romano Guardini suggests it does. Though the term "environmentalism" did not exist in the early twentieth century, I think it is fair to count Guardini's short book from 1926, *Letters from Lake Como*, as a foundational text of a tradition of authentically Catholic "environmentalism." Born in Italy yet raised in Germany, Guardini wrote these letters as a series of reflections inspired by his visit to his mother who had retired to her family's ancestral home in the beautiful mountain district of Lake Como in northern Italy. In contrast to the modern industrial world of Germany, Lake Como struck Guardini as in some respects a throwback to an earlier time, a kind of pre-modern, pre-industrial Eden that had somehow escaped the ravages of modern industrial development. Still, Guardini was no naïve romantic. He recognized that industrial modernity was slowly making its presence felt even at Lake Como and used this observable contrast between pre-industrial and industrial relations to the natural world as a way of reflecting on the proper relation of man not simply to the natural environment, but to his fellow man and to God.

Before I turn to Guardini proper, I wish to clarify what I mean by an authentically Catholic environmentalism. To say that there is a distinctly Catholic environmentalism is not necessarily to dismiss non-Catholic environmental thought. Pope Francis has recently reminded us that good evangelists build bridges, not walls. I believe that the environmental movement presents a tremendous opportunity for evangelism in that loving concern for God's creation offers a potentially powerful common ground uniting Catholics with non-Catholics. Still, we see challenges even at the basic definition of this common ground. What do we love? The "environment" or "God's creation"? These terms are neither neutral nor interchangeable. Each of them contains an implicit world view with very particular assumptions about how we relate to the natural world, to each other and to God.

Catholics concerned for God's creation have been all too willing to adopt a secular language of "environmentalism" in the spirit of building coalitions with non-Catholics. Such coalition building is good in itself, but with respect to the environment/creation, it has been a necessity due to the virtual non-existence of a distinctly Catholic movement. There is no necessary spiritual or intellectual reason for this state of affairs. The official statements of the Church touching on environmental issues over the last fifty years can be interpreted as nothing other than "green" friendly. Still, environmentalists have often been hostile to the Church. In general, environmentalists have often blamed the Book of Genesis for inspiring an exploitative attitude toward nature that really derives more from modern science than biblical theology. More specifically, environmentalists often condemn the Church's opposition to artificial birth control as criminally irresponsible and contributing to the destruction of nature through overpopulation. In this cultural context, the bridges between Catholic and non-Catholic environmentalists have too often been one-way streets, with Catholics growing more distant from their Church as they grow closer to nature.

The danger here, moreover, is less secularism than a new kind of paganism. Despite the current anxiety over global warming, few people are drawn to the environmental movement in response to the latest findings of science. Environmentalism has become a new kind of nature worship, often tied to old philosophies and world views rooted in non-Western cultures, be they Native American or East Asian. On this issue, I can speak from experience. I grew up in the 1960s and saw many of my older brothers and sisters drawn out of the faith by the hippie counterculture, which seemed to offer a more spiritual and natural way of living. As I came of high school and college age in the late 1970s and 1980s, I saw this attraction passed on to the youth of my generation, and I know it is still very much alive today. We all know the type of rock star who declares himself a Buddhist and works to support the environment. The general perception in popular youth culture is that if you care about the environment, you should reject Christianity, or at the very least every organized, institutional expression of Christianity. Despite all of the official hostility to the Church among political leaders of the Western world, the Church still appears to many young people as part of the establishment, and to be young is to rebel against the establishment.

Well, what does Romano Guardini have to say to all of this? First, a little biographical background. Although he came of age nearly a hundred years ago, he is in some sense our contemporary in that he grew up in a culture that was, like our own, hostile to the Church. Born in 1885 in Verona, Italy, Guardini soon moved with his family to the city of Mainz, in Germany where his father went in search of employment. His parents were faithful, if not excessively devout, Catholics who raised Guardini with a love for the great classics of European humanism, ranging from Dante's *Divine Comedy* to Goethe's *Faust*. By the early twentieth century, however, science had eclipsed literary humanism as the great achievement of European civilization. Indeed, for the enlightened of that age, modern science had rendered traditional Christianity obsolete. Guardini tried to embrace the spirit of his age through the study of chemistry and economics. Attending the University of Munich, he noticed that many of his fellow students had abandoned their religious beliefs; this caused him to begin to question his own faith. Guardini then underwent a period of spiritual crisis that he would later compare to that of St. Augustine. He emerged from this crisis with a renewed faith but continued to pursue his secular studies. Still, after a few months of studying economics at the University of Berlin, he felt the call to the priesthood, eventually receiving holy orders on May 28, 1910. Over the next ten years, Guardini pursued a Ph.D. that would qualify him to teach in the German university system, served two years of service as a hospital orderly for the German army during World War I, and held various parish assignments.

It was Guardini's parish work, rather than his academic study, that led most directly to his writing *Letters from Lake Como*. The letters had originally appeared in the journal *Schidgenossen*, the house organ for Quickborn, the national Catholic youth association of Germany. Guardini had been chaplain to the diocesan youth group in Mainz since the beginning of his parish assignments in 1915. Quickborn means "wellspring of life," and I think that this gives you some sense of the broad vision of Catholic youth groups at the time. When I was growing up, Catholic youth ministry meant pretty much sports (CYO basketball) and any activity that would keep teenagers busy and out of trouble, particularly trouble of a sexual nature. The youth organizations that swept across the Western world in the late nineteenth and early-twentieth centuries were actually in part a response to the very sort of issues that would later give birth to the environmental movement. Even the most enthusiastic supporters of material and scientific progress recognized that there was something profoundly unnatural and alienating about modern industrial life. Political and cultural leaders of the time felt that the distance from nature demanded by modern industrial life would somehow stunt or distort the natural development of youth. So too, the breakup of the home economy destroyed the traditional skills and responsibilities that parents passed on to their children as part of their education to adulthood. Schools replaced parents as educators but did little to bring students into the contact with nature, even though deemed essential to healthy growth and development. In the English-speaking world, this concern expressed itself in the rise of the Scouting movement.

Sharing common concerns, Guardini nonetheless offers a distinct response. Against the Anglo-American-Protestant tendency to view nature as uninhabited wilderness, Guardini experiences the natural beauty of Lake Como as inextricably bound up with human culture. Guardini's first letter, titled "The Question," raises the issue of the meaning of industrialism as it has spread into a previously unindustrialized region of Italy. He frames the problem in the following way: "I saw machines invading the land that had previously been the home of culture."[1] Significantly, he criticizes industrialism as less a corruption of pure nature than a transformation of culture. Though Guardini constantly scolds himself for lapsing into romanticism and nostalgia, this opening observation marks his distance from the most pernicious form of environmental romanticism, the ideal of pure nature.

Nature was made for human habitation. The question is not whether to interact with nature or leave it alone, but how to live with nature in a manner that is both human and natural. Despite the inroads of industrialism, Guardini encountered in Italy the survival of authentic culture understood as a healthy relationship between man and nature:

As I walked through the valleys of Brianza, from Milan to Lake Como, luxuriant, cultivated with zealous industry, encircled by austere mountains, broad and powerful, I could not believe my eyes. Everywhere it was an inhabited land, valleys and slopes dotted with hamlets and small towns. All nature had been given a new shape by us humans. What culture means in its narrowest sense struck me with full force. The lines of the roofs merged from different directions. They went through the small town set on the hillside or followed the windings of a valley. Integrated in many ways, they finally reached a climax in the belfry with its deep-toned bell. All these things were caught up and encircled by the well-constructed mountain masses. Culture, very lofty and yet self-sufficient, very naturally—I have no other word.

1 Romano Guardini, *Letters from Lake Como: Explorations in Technology and the Human Race* (Grand Rapids: W. B. Eerdmans, 1994), 5. All future references to this work will be by page number in parentheses following the quote or paraphrase.

Nature, then has been reshaped, subjected to mind and spirit, yet it is perfectly simple.... Here nature can pass over smoothly into culture. There is nothing alien or *antithetical* to culture that must wither away if this humanity, this *urbanitas*, this art of living is to come into being. I cannot find a way to express how human this nature is and how we feel in it the possibility of being human in a totally clear but inexhaustibly profound sense.

Yet all at once, then, on the singing lines of a small town, I saw the great box of a factory. (5–6)

Guardini clearly presents the "great box of a factory" as an intrusion, a violation of sorts, but he sets this against "the singing lines of a small town," not pristine, uninhabited nature.

The box shape of the factory contrasts with the "lines of the roofs" that merged "in different directions," "integrated" and reaching a "climax in the belfry with its deep-toned bell." The bell tower of a pre-industrial town would in most cases be connected to a church. Here Guardini implicitly comments on the way that the factory whistle had come to replace the church bell as society's time keeper. Modern industrialism in this way usurped the cultural authority of the Church in ways that affected people much more directly than the criticisms leveled against the Church by skeptical, secular intellectuals.

Guardini acknowledges that many might find his critique of factories as a romantic luxury insensitive to the stark economic realities facing poor Italians with few employment options. Sympathetic to the plight of the poor, Guardini nonetheless insists on the need to make real distinctions between what is natural and unnatural in man's relationship to nature. In his second letter, "Artificiality of Existence," he contrasts an ocean liner and a sailboat. The ocean liner is a tremendous technical achievement, but the achievement lies in creating an artificial distance between man and the sea. The great boast of many cruise ships today is, somewhat paradoxically, that you can be on a cruise and hardly know that you are at sea; the ocean is reduced to scenery and salt air. Contrast this with the physical reality of a sailboat:

The lines and proportions of the ship are still in profound harmony with the pressure of the wind and waves and the vital human measure. Those who control this ship are still very closely related to the wind and the waves.

We have here real culture—elevation above nature, yet decisive nearness to it. We are still in a vital way body, but we are shot through with mind and spirit. We master nature by the power of mind and spirit, but we ourselves remain natural. (12)

Other contrasts include the horse-drawn plow vs. the tractor, an open-hearth cooking vs. a coal stove, and candle light vs. electricity. In all of these developments, Guardini sees our experience of life becoming increasingly abstract and distanced from nature.

Guardini was neither the first nor the last to make these criticisms of industrialism. This type of critique can be difficult to read for people who happen, through no fault of their own, to live at a certain remove from nature—that is, for the vast majority of people in the developed world. How are we to respond? What are we to do? Go sailing? Work on a farm? Abstain from electricity? Most of us are not in a position to practice this type of extreme renunciation. But here is where Guardini's emphasis on culture opens up other possibilities. The unnatural relation between man and nature extends to social and economic relations among people. The factories that destroy nature also introduce an unnatural relation of production and consumption into human society. Against theorists such as Adam Smith, Guardini sees capitalism destroying "the organic interplay of supply and demand," creating a system of "unlimited production" in which "every art of force and cunning must be used to produce unlimited consumption" (58). This is where most of us experience the assault on nature most directly, but where the assault is perhaps least apparent. Many of us have some vague awareness that all the mass-produced junk we consume is produced in far away factories that probably harm nature, not to mention the factory workers. Yet the rage for "clean energy" and "sustainability" suggests that we miss the assault on nature right in front of our eyes, represented by the consumption-on-demand mentality of our society.

The post-industrial, high-tech economies of today far outpace the older industrial models in the incitement of insatiable desire—just think of the internet. We now expect everything from pornography to EWTN to be just a click away on our computer. Hardly any of the consumer goods that drive our economy are essential; most of them are positively harmful to proper human flourishing. A Catholic environmentalism could well begin with a heroic, but ultimately quite practical, detachment from consumerism. This detachment would entail less a renunciation of desire than a discovery of true desire and true need. To use one of Guardini's metaphors, this detachment would enable us to become true sailors of desire, learning to listen to and conform ourselves to the authentic, God-given needs present in our bodies and souls.

Detachment, yes. But what are we going to do with all that free time? Well, Guardini saw this problem even back in the 1920s. Mass production and consumption had so distorted natural human living that people were nearly unable to imagine any other way of living: the artificial had become natural. In his seventh letter, titled "The Masses," Guardini observed: "How we long for an arcane discipline that will protect what is sacred from the marketplace, including the marketplace within" (60). Guardini could say this because he in fact spent most of his life as a priest developing such a discipline. That discipline is the liturgy. Though Guardini's *Letters from Lake Como* offers invaluable insights into man's relationship with creation, his first and still best known book, *The Spirit of the Liturgy* (1918), sought to bring man into a closer and more authentic relation with his Creator.[2] Guardini's writing on the liturgy is rich and complex, and I can only skim the surface of it here. With respect to the themes of nature and culture in *Letters from Lake Como*, I think one of the most import points of contact is Guardini's insistence that liturgy is the expression of a communal,

2 Romano Guardini, *The Spirit of the Liturgy* (New York: Crossroad Publishers, 1998).

rather than individual, reverence for God. To be fair, Guardini thought that the average Catholic Mass of the early twentieth century also failed to satisfy this desire. Hardly anyone could understand Latin and bilingual missals were rare. Few people received communion on a regular basis; even the most devout tended to spend most of their time at Mass reciting private prayers and devotions rather than following what the prayers of the priest as he celebrated the Mass. Following the exhortation of no less a figure than Pius X, Guardini wrote of the need to develop a more active, conscious participation by the laity at Mass. Guardini dedicated much of his work with the Catholic youth organization Quickborn to introducing youth to some of the liturgical innovation being conducted in Benedictine monasteries in France and Germany.

Today, liturgy may not seem to offer much potential as a unifying cultural alternative to secular consumerism and neo-pagan environmentalism. Among many Catholics, it is a cause for indifference; among the committed few, has been an occasion for total war. The liturgical documents of the Second Vatican Council reflect many of Guardini's ideas of communal, active participation, yet Guardini was deeply troubled by what he saw taking place in the name of liturgical renewal in the middle of the 1960s. Despite his concern to foster conscious participation and emotional engagement in the liturgy, he saw in post-Vatican II liturgical reform an explosion of new forms of the spiritual individualism he had long argued against. The communal fellowship of the liturgy required a type of a surrender of independence that was anathema to the post-Vatican II generation. The Gospel truth that in order to save your life, you must first lose it, has never been an easy teaching to accept, much less understand.

Again, this is not the place to go into the particulars of Guardini's understanding of the liturgy. The immediate task before us is simply to put liturgy at the center of our cultural life. Pay attention to and observe the liturgical calendar. Pray the Liturgy of the Hours. Go to daily Mass. I try to do all these things. They remain a great mystery to me. But whether I understand them fully or not, I am at least directing my attention toward God and the communion of saints rather than surfing the internet or pursuing some solitary communion with nature. Structured as it is according to the hours of the day and the days of the year, the liturgy is the most ecological of cultural practices. It instills an awareness of and submission to the natural rhythms of life that in the long run will do more to save the environment than any orchestrated media spectacle.

Though I would like to hold up liturgy as an authentically Catholic ecological practice, I realize it presents certain dangers. In Guardini's time as in our own, there is always the romantic temptation to turn to liturgy, as to nature, as a retreat from the harsh realities of the modern world. I would like to conclude with a few words of caution from Guardini himself:

> We must not oppose what is new and try to preserve a beautiful world that is inevitably perishing. Nor should we try to build a new world of the creative imagination that will show none of the damage of what is actually evolving. Rather, we must transform what is coming to be. But we can do this only if we honestly say yes to it and yet with incorruptible hearts remain aware of all that is destructive and nonhuman in it. Our age has been given to us as the soil on which to stand and the task to master. (80-81)

5

Catholicism and the Natural World

COMMENTARY ON THE CATECHISM OF THE CATHOLIC CHURCH, NUMBERS 337–344 & 2415–2418

THOMAS STORCK

T HE *CATECHISM OF THE CATHOLIC Church* has proved a helpful summary of the Church's faith, not only for potential converts, but also for instructing those who are already Catholics, who in view of the widespread crisis of belief that has followed the Second Vatican Council are greatly in need of an authoritative restatement of their religion. For unless Catholics are catechized by the Church, they will assuredly be catechized by the world. Our minds are continually being formed, or misformed, and it is the ideas that result from this that ultimately govern our conduct. As Father John Hardon has written, "All the evil in the world begins with error. Or, more personally, all sin in the human heart begins as untruth in the human mind."[1] Too often we take in uncritically notions from the culture around us, many of which are at variance with Catholic truth. In the turmoil occasioned by the Council, catechetics has declined to the point that very many Catholics have little or no knowledge of their religion, but even among those Catholics who take pains to preserve their orthodoxy there are generally areas in which the ideas that govern their actions are not in accord with the teaching of the Church. This is most likely to occur in matters where we are scarcely aware that there is any authoritative Catholic teaching, especially in

---

1 John A. Hardon, *Spiritual Life in the Modern World* (Boston: St. Paul Editions, c. 1982), p. 36.

those areas which transcend personal and individual morality and concern mankind organized as a community, such as the morality of economic life. It is such a subject that I wish to take up here, namely the question of our proper attitude and conduct toward the natural order, toward the created or natural environment around us. In this area, as in so many others, it seems that the Devil sponsors two opposite errors, for the world offers us two competing outlooks, both of which are wrong. In reacting against the one that seems most wrong to us, we are apt to embrace the other, so, for example, as we rightly reject the New Age pantheistic account of nature, we are in danger of embracing an ideology rooted in Cartesianism or Deism, which is equally opposed both to the explicit teaching of the Church as well as to the perennial philosophy of St. Thomas Aquinas. The remedy for this is knowledge, knowledge of what the Church teaches in these areas, and a docile spirit toward her authority. Here therefore I will explicate certain paragraphs of the *Catechism* that deal with the visible created order or the natural environment, and man's relations with that order. We will see that there is definite Catholic teaching on this subject and thus a distinct Catholic way of dealing with it. And far from being something remote from our lives, this teaching is in fact of great importance for how we live, and especially for how our society conducts itself.

The *Catechism*'s initial discussion of the natural creation takes place within its exposition of the Creed or Profession of Faith. After speaking of God as "Creator of heaven and earth" and of "all that is seen and unseen" (325), it then goes on to speak of the angelic order, and finally of the visible world. Let us look at the paragraphs that deal with this.

> No. 337. God himself created the visible world in all its richness, diversity, and order. Scripture presents the work of the Creator symbolically as a succession of six days of divine "work," concluded by the "rest" of the seventh day. On the subject of creation, the sacred text teaches the truths revealed by God for our salvation, permitting us to "recognize the inner nature, the value, and the ordering of the whole of creation to the praise of God."

No. 338. *Nothing exists that does not owe its existence to God the Creator.* The world began when God's word drew it out of nothingness; all existent beings, all of nature, and all human history are rooted in this primordial event, the very genesis by which the world was constituted and time begun.

One of the major points separating Catholics, and indeed all Christians, as well as Jews and Muslims, from much of the rest of the world, is the question of creation. Where did the perceptible world about us come from? In antiquity many people held that the world had always existed, or that the world was an *emanation from* God, not a creation by God. This latter is akin to pantheism, the belief that the world is a part of God or indistinguishable from God. Today Hinduism and other east Asian religions, for example, either explicitly or implicitly accept pantheism,[2] and contemporary New Age writers usually embrace similar ideas.[3] Even the current scientific theory of the Big Bang, though it has certain resemblances to the idea of a creation, supposes something to have existed before the Big Bang, and thus, unlike what is required by the Catholic faith, it is not creation out of nothing.[4]

2 "God and the Self are one.... God dwells within you always. Furthermore, if you look carefully within yourself at the in-dwelling Lord, you'll discover that you are nothing but *that* — that your body is nothing but a coalescing of that divine, creative power." Comparing us and the Divine to waves and the ocean, the author continues: "You arise and subside quickly — just like that — out of, and back into, the Divine." And a little later: "... the essence of all Life is really only one thing." Swami Chetanananda, *The Breath of God* (Portland, Oregon: Rudra Press, c. 1988), pp. 2–4.

3 "Because the goddess is portrayed as an immanent deity, one who is in nature and inseparable from it, it is not transparently clear how she could have created it. And indeed, creation stories play a less important role in feminist spirituality than they do in many other religions. On the rare occasions when a creation story is told, it is a story of birth." Cynthia Eller, *Living in the Lap of the Goddess: The Feminist Spirituality Movement in America* (New York: Crossroad, c. 1993), p. 138.

4 Pope John Paul II in fact warned against "making uncritical and overhasty use for apologetic purposes of such recent theories as that of the 'Big Bang' in cosmology." Letter to Rev. George V. Coyne, S. J., Director of the Vatican Observatory, June 1, 1988. Available at *http://www.vatican.va/content/john-paul-ii/en/letters/1988/documents/hf_jp-ii_let_19880601_padre-coyne.html* Accessed August 22, 2020.

While rejecting pantheism, or any notion that the world is an emanation from God, we must also reject Deism. Superficially the Deistic concept of creation looks like the Catholic concept, but in fact they are essentially different. The paradigm of Deistic creation and the Deistic God is the Watchmaker. Though sometimes used by Protestant Christians, and even by Catholics, the notion of God as the watchmaker has serious defects for a true Theism, since the God of Deism is essentially one who creates, but then walks away from his creation, while the true God, the God both of genuine philosophy and of Abraham, Isaac and Jacob, both creates and continuously upholds his creation in being. As Ronald Knox wrote,

> Paley's metaphor of the watch once for all wound up is, of course, the classic illustration of this Deist conception. It represents God as having made the universe, but not as guiding it from moment to moment, still less as actually holding it in being.[5]

A better (but still inadequate) physical image for God and his creation than the watchmaker and the watch is the electric generator and the light bulb, for the light bulb depends on the generator not only for the beginning of its operation but also for its continuing to provide light, while the watchmaker makes the watch, winds it up, and then is free to go away.

Moreover, the concept of miracles was difficult or impossible to fit into the Deistic universe, for if their God simply made the watch, wound it up and went away, how could the course of this mechanical creation ever deviate from its predetermined path? Even the idea of God's providence, of God hearing and answering our prayers, while perhaps not absolutely incompatible with Deism,[6] is foreign to its spirit, for it is hard to see how the Deistic God has any continuing interest in his workmanship. And though Deism is a heresy most characteristic of the eighteenth century, *Deistic attitudes are still active today, as we will see below.*

---

5   *The Belief of Catholics* (Garden City, N.Y.: Image, 1958), pp. 62–63.
6   One can argue that even the deistic God, being outside of time, perhaps could have arranged his creation from the beginning to take account of the prayers that would later be addressed to him.

Although the *Catechism* speaks of the "six days" of creation, this of course does not commit a Catholic to a literal naïve reading of the early chapters of Genesis.[7] Protestant fundamentalists hold that the six days of Genesis must be interpreted literally, and as a result they reject the theory of the evolution of all organic beings from one or a few primeval one-celled creatures taking place over long aeons of time. Catholics have never been required to accept such an interpretation of Genesis. However, the question of evolution, or, more properly, macroevolution, is logically distinct from this and must be decided on the scientific evidence. One could reject both the fundamentalist view of Genesis and macroevolution at the same time. This point is outside the scope of this book, however.

> **No. 339.** *Each creature possesses its own particular goodness and perfection.* For each one of the works of the "six days" it is said: "And God saw that it was good." "By the very nature of creation, material being is endowed with its own stability, truth, and excellence, its own order and laws." Each of the various creatures, willed in its own being, reflects in its own way a ray of God's infinite wisdom and goodness. Man must therefore respect the particular goodness of every creature, to avoid any disordered use of things which would be in contempt of the Creator and would bring disastrous consequences for human beings and their environment.

"Each creature possesses its own particular goodness and perfection" and "Each of the various creatures, willed in its own being, reflects in its own way a ray of God's infinite wisdom and goodness." In these two sentences we have a perfect summary of the Catholic doctrine on and attitude toward the created order of natures. Without denying that mankind is

---

7 Among many possible sources, see the decisions of the Pontifical Biblical Commission, "On the Historical Character of the First Three Chapters of Genesis," June 30, 1909, especially nos. 7 and 8; and the letter of the Pontifical Biblical Commission to Cardinal Suhard, Archbishop of Paris, on the literary form of the first eleven chapters of Genesis, January 16, 1948, both reprinted in *Rome and the Study of Scripture* (St. Meinrad, Indiana: Grail, rev. ed. 1962), pp. 122–24, 150–153.

the crown and ruler of creation, nevertheless the individual beings of the plant and animal kingdoms, even rocks and minerals, have a perfection of their own and reflect "a ray of God's infinite wisdom and goodness."

As St. Thomas Aquinas explains, something is called bad only if it lacks what is proper to it, "as a man is called bad insofar as he lacks virtue, and an eye is called bad insofar as it lacks sharpness of sight."[8] We call a car that runs well, for example, a good car, and one whose engine is broken, bad (not morally bad, of course). So therefore everything that God has created has its own goodness, simply in itself, regardless of how it may benefit mankind. But if we forget this truth, we are apt to take a view of the rest of creation that looks on it much as a Deist might—they are simply external objects, like the watch, with no relation to God. For if the watchmaker simply makes the watch and then goes away, the watch not only displays no dependence on its maker, and thus no special relation to him, but is simply a neutral object which we may treat any way we choose. The watch is an essentially secular object, that is, divorced from God. In the Deistic universe, the world of natures is a world (apart from its origins) that exists on its own. Its God is far from it, and it awaits (should we so choose) our exploitation.

In a volume that contains much just criticism of the Green movement's attitudes toward man and the natural order, *The Cross and the Rain Forest*, two of the book's authors, Robert Whelan and Joseph Kirwan, seem to regard the natural order in this Deistic way. Whelan criticizes those who regard a tree "as more than just a source of wood," and Kirwan seems to raise difficulties over whether animals should be called "creatures" or simply "things."[9] These sorts of attitudes have been common in the Western world for some time, even among those, such as Catholics, who should have known better, and since error tends to breed error, the reaction against the Deistic way of looking at the earth and the other creatures who live on it is in large part the reason for the absurdities and immoralities of

8 *Summa Theologiae*, I, q. 5, a. 3.
9 Grand Rapids, Mich.: Acton Institute, c. 1996, pp. 40 and 114–15.

the Green and other movements that reject traditional Christianity.[10] As Catholics we must try to make our attitude toward our fellow creatures that of Holy Scripture, which eloquently speaks of animals, plants and even ice and snow or clouds and lightning, as praising God simply by their existence.[11]

> **No. 340.** God wills the *interdependence of creatures*. The sun and the moon, the cedar and the little flower, the eagle and the sparrow: the spectacle of their countless diversities and inequalities tells us that no creature is self-sufficient. Creatures exist only in dependence on each other, to complete each other, in the service of each other.

The system of "interdependence of creatures" is what we generally call nature. Nature is simply the system of nature*s*. Each created thing, sun and moon, large tree and little flower, has what we call a nature, that is, a whatness: each is a distinct and different kind of thing. As we saw above, it is by being itself, in its own integrity, that a thing is good. But none of these individual goods exists entirely by or for itself, "no creature is self-sufficient." Thus even though each created thing praises God simply by existing, they also exist "in the service of each other." Plants make use of the sun, rain and minerals

10 In *Living in the Lap of the Goddess*, Cynthia Eller quotes Elizabeth Dodson Gray on "patriarchal religion." "The goal of this old 'sacred game' is to get away from the ordinary, the natural, the 'unsacred' — away from women, fleshly bodies, decaying nature, away from all that is rooted in mortality and dying. 'Up, up and away' is the cry of this religious consciousness as it seeks to ascend to the elevated realm of pure spirit and utter transcendence where nothing gets soiled, or rots, or dies" (p. 136). Here is a mistaken identification between Deism and true Christianity. The God of Catholicism took flesh in the womb of a woman, nursed at her breasts, lived among us, sanctified a marriage feast by changing water into wine, and died a horrible death on a cross, his body smeared with sweat and blood. To the extent that Catholics have failed to emphasize the "earthy" aspects of the Faith, we seem to have nothing to offer to those who rightly disdain a religion of "pure spirit and utter transcendence." One obvious antidote to such an over-spiritual Catholicism is meditation on the mysteries of the Rosary, all of which, in one way or another, are concerned with earthly life, the body, conception, birth or death. The Rosary surely exhibits a religion that is very much involved with what "gets soiled or rots or dies."

11 See especially Psalm 148 and Daniel 3:57–81.

from the soil; animals eat plants and other animals and use wood or grass or sand to make nests or other dwellings. So while it is good to allow animals and plants to live their own life, for of themselves they praise God, it is also good to cut down trees to construct buildings needed for mankind's use or to eat plants and animals, since they exist also to serve us and each other. According to the Deistic concept of creation, created things would exist *solely* for our use, and even for our misuse. But since each created thing praises God by being itself, we cannot use them except in our genuine service and for our genuine welfare. It is as if we employed a servant who, whenever he was not actually serving us, spent his time worshipping before the Blessed Sacrament. Would we dare call him from this holy work to help us in something immoral or even frivolous? We can consider our use of the natural world analogously. Since each created thing blesses and praises God in its natural state, simply by existing, we ought not to take away that praise from God unless we have good reason. For natural things are not simply at our disposal, but exist "to complete each other, in the service of each other." If we use them for frivolous reasons, or for things which ultimately are harmful to human society, then we are not using them in our service, but to our hurt. The mere piling up of consumer goods, the spending of huge sums on unworthy objects, our insatiable appetite for amusements — are any of these sufficiently important to justify our taking away things of the natural order from their work of praising God? As Pope John Paul wrote in *Centesimus Annus*:

> It is not wrong to want to live better; what is wrong
> is a style of life which is presumed to be better when
> it is directed towards "having" rather than "being,"
> and which wants to have more, not in order to be
> more but in order to spend life in enjoyment as an
> end in itself. (no. 36)

The gravity of sin involved in misusing natural objects doubtless depends on many factors, but one can hardly deny the existence of some sin.

No. 341. *The beauty of the universe*: The order and harmony of the created world results from the diversity of beings and from the relationships which exist among them. Man discovers them progressively as the laws of nature. They call forth the admiration of scholars. The beauty of creation reflects the infinite beauty of the Creator and ought to inspire the respect and submission of man's intellect and will.

The *Catechism* here reflects what men for centuries have concluded when they examined carefully the cosmos. Aristotle wrote concerning knowledge of animals:

> For if some [animals] have no graces to charm the sense, yet even these, by disclosing to intellectual perception the artistic spirit that designed them, give immense pleasure to all who can trace links of causation, and are inclined to philosophy.[12]

This ability to "trace links of causation," as well as our perception of the "beauty of creation" ought to lead any unprejudiced person to recognize "the infinite beauty of the Creator," and further "ought to inspire the respect and submission of [his] intellect and will." As St. Paul wrote,

> For what can be known about God is plain to them, because God has shown it to them. Ever since the creation of the world his invisible nature, namely, his eternal power and deity, has been clearly perceived in the things that have been made. (Rom. 1:19-20)

The fact that many today see the things that God has made and yet, not being able or willing to "trace links of causation," fail to see the Creator, certainly calls into question our notion of the superiority of our civilization over all past ages. Centuries of bad philosophy and bad education have rendered modern man less capable of true philosophical insight and perception of beauty than our supposedly rude ancestors. A comparison between a church built in the Middle Ages and most churches built in the last forty or fifty years should be sufficient to show which civilization is really superior.

12 *On the Parts of Animals*, bk. I, 5.

No. 342. The *hierarchy of creatures* is expressed by the order of the "six days," from the less perfect to the more perfect. God loves all his creatures and takes care of each one, even the sparrow. Nevertheless, Jesus said: "You are of more value than many sparrows," or again: "Of how much more value is a man than a sheep!"

No. 343. *Man is the summit* of the Creator's work, as the inspired account expresses by clearly distinguishing the creation of man from that of the other creatures.

It is necessary to make very careful distinctions in commenting on these passages in order to avoid the errors which lurk on each side of truth. On the one hand are those who deny that man has any special place in creation. For example, the organization Earth First!, in one of its proposals stated that

> the central idea of Earth First! is that humans have no divine right to subdue the Earth, that we are merely one of several million forms of life on this planet. We reject even the notion of benevolent stewardship as that implies dominance.[13]

In 1987 two Earth First! members held up a banner at the Lincoln Memorial in Washington, D. C. that proclaimed "EQUAL RIGHTS FOR ALL SPECIES."[14] Such notions, if interpreted literally, are contrary to what God has revealed. But I fear that in some cases people have reacted not against the

13 Quoted in Christopher Manes, *Green Rage: Radical Environmentalism and the Unmaking of Civilization* (Boston: Little, Brown, c. 1990), p. 74.

14 *Ibid.*, p. 166. In fact, certain thinkers have gone beyond the idea of equal rights for all species to condemn the very existence of mankind. In an article on the American poet Robinson Jeffers (1887–1962) the writer notes Jeffers' sentiment "that the world would be better off without us," and adds as his own comment: "It's a sentiment to which I have become deeply sympathetic.... Which is another way of saying that it wouldn't bother me in the least if the entire human race vanished from the face of the earth, along with its architecture and literature and military gunships. Good riddance to us all." Erik Reece, "Bright Power, Dark Peace: Robinson Jeffers and the Hope of Human Extinction," *Harper's Magazine*, vol. 341, no. 2044, September 2020, pp. 52–59, at p. 58.

Catholic and biblical teaching on man's place in the cosmos but against a distorted version of it. The Deistic deformation of truth seemed to allow mankind to do absolutely anything to the earth and the other creatures living on it, with no object except man's short-term gain. This of course is not what the Church teaches, as the *Catechism* makes very clear, for the fact that man is the "*summit* of the Creator's work" does not mean that everything he desires to do with the natural world is good or permissible. For the desires that flow from the heart of fallen man are not all for the good or for the glory of God. Therefore we cannot cloak our frequent misuse of the natural creation under the truth that we have been commanded by God to subdue the earth, for God has not given us authority to do absolutely anything we may want with the created cosmos.

> No. 344. There is a *solidarity among all creatures* arising from the fact that all have the same Creator and are all ordered to his glory.[15]

In human affairs solidarity is equated with social charity by Pope John Paul II.[16] Obviously we cannot have charity toward plants or irrational animals, but we can have something akin or analogous to it. We can treat them as, in a way, our brothers who join us in praising God and "are all ordered to his glory." That is, instead of looking on the natural world as something alien or other, something neutral or passive, something waiting for us to use or shape, we can see that world as alive with praise of God. This is not pantheism or an unChristian worship of the natural order. It is simply a realization of what is proclaimed in Holy Scripture and explicitly reiterated in the *Catechism*. Again, this does not mean that we cannot use these natural creatures and objects, but it does mean that even as we use we ought to use with reverence, we ought to realize that they are ordered not just to our use and benefit but directly to God also. In a personal account of the killing of a pig in the Shenandoah Valley of

---

15 This *Catechism* paragraph concludes with a quotation from St. Francis which is omitted here on account of its length.
16 Encyclical *Centesimus Annus*, no. 10. See also the *Catechism*, no. 1939, where it is also equated with friendship.

Virginia, William Fahey wrote of having a priest bless the animal before it was slaughtered.

'I thought it right to have Father bless the pig and our work.' More than a few dry throats swallowed before the old man spoke. 'You did right there, John (for that was my friend's name). My father always, always blessed the pig, or had it done. It is a pig, but it is a life. There's no sense in doing something without gratitude. That's just plain ignorant.'[17]

Thus we can speak of a true solidarity of creatures, a solidarity that will be ultimately crowned when "all things are subjected to him" and "the Son himself will also be subjected to him who put all things under him, that God may be everything to every one" (I Cor. 15:28).[18]

Let us now look at a later section in the *Catechism* which takes up the topic of man's treatment of the natural world in more detail and from the standpoint of the commandments.

No. 2415. The seventh commandment enjoins respect for the integrity of creation. Animals, like plants and inanimate beings, are by nature destined for the common good of past, present, and future humanity. Use of the mineral, vegetable, and animal resources of the universe cannot be divorced from respect for moral imperatives. Man's dominion over inanimate and other living beings granted by the Creator is not absolute; it is limited by concern for the quality of life of his neighbor, including generations to come; it requires a religious respect for the integrity of creation.

No. 2416. *Animals* are God's creatures. He surrounds them with his providential care. By their mere existence they bless him and give him glory. Thus men owe them kindness. We should recall

17 William Fahey, "For the Life of this Pig," in Tobias Lanz, ed., *Beyond Capitalism and Socialism: a New Statement of an Old Ideal* (Norfolk: Light in the Darkness Publications, 2008), p. 138

18 One can also see our Lady's Assumption and Coronation as a kind of crowning of the natural order, for her body was nourished by the plants and animals of the created cosmos.

the gentleness with which saints like St. Francis of Assisi or St. Philip Neri treated animals.

No. 2417. God entrusted animals to the stewardship of those whom he created in his own image. Hence it is legitimate to use animals for food and clothing. They may be domesticated to help man in his work and leisure. Medical and scientific experimentation on animals is a morally acceptable practice if it remains within reasonable limits and contributes to caring for or saving human lives.

No. 2418. It is contrary to human dignity to cause animals to suffer or die needlessly. It is likewise unworthy to spend money on them that should as a priority go to the relief of human misery. One can love animals; one should not direct to them the affection due only to persons.

This second set of paragraphs is from part three of the Catechism, "Life in Christ," which deals with Christian moral life. The paragraphs here are from a discussion of the Seventh Commandment, You Shall Not Steal. For to misuse any created thing is surely to take what does not belong to us, since all creation belongs to God and is granted to us for our use, not our misuse.

This section of the Catechism sets forth the dual truth about created natures: they have an integrity, and thus a goodness, of their own, "their mere existence" blesses and glorifies God, but yet at the same time they are "entrusted ... to [our] stewardship" and "destined for the common good of ... humanity." The limits of our use of animals, and even plants, however, lie not only in the effect of such use on mankind, but in "a religious respect for the integrity of creation," and in the kindness we "owe" them. We may safely assume, however, that we are not violating this "kindness" as long as we use animals and plants for the true welfare of mankind. But the mere piling up of goods, as we saw above, is likely to be a misuse rather than a use.

And unfortunately, this is exactly what modern man does. For example, in the United States, as average family size has declined, the average size of new houses built has increased.

In 1970 the average size of a new single-family home was 1500 square feet; by 2019 it had increased to 2301square feet. In 1970 the average family size was 3.58 persons; in 2019 it was 3.14 persons.[19] In many other areas what our fathers considered luxuries are now items of daily use, or have even been surpassed. In fact, our economic system requires such a continual and irrational consuming in order to stave off economic disaster, and unless corporate profits are increasing, businessmen are likely to be dissatisfied. But I fear that most of us do not even think to include these sorts of things in an examination of conscience, forgetting St. Paul's dictum, "There is great gain in godliness with contentment; for we brought nothing into the world, and we cannot take anything out of the world; but if we have food and clothing, with these we shall be content" (I Tim. 6:6-8). Those of us who have much more than "food and clothing," perhaps should be content with *that*.

> The Catechism states that "Medical and scientific experimentation on animals is a morally acceptable practice if it remains within reasonable limits and contributes to caring for or saving human lives." Yet many experiments on animals are conducted not for saving lives, but for testing cosmetics. It would seem hard to reconcile this kind of testing, which is often very cruel, with the "solidarity" and the "kindness" we should have for animals.[20]

The principles that ought to govern our attitude and conduct toward the created order of natures that are stated in the

19 1970 data from *Statistical Abstract of the United States, 1997* (Washington: Government Printing Office, 1997), tables 66 and 1187. 2019 data from U. S. Census Bureau, Characteristics of New Housing, https://www.census.gov/construction/chars/highlights.html and U. S. Census Bureau, Historical Household Tables, https://www.census.gov/data/tables/time-series/demo/families/households.html Accessed August 22, 2020.

20 Even Joseph Kirwan, one of the authors I criticized above for having an attitude toward the created order akin to Deism, opines that experimentation on animals "for cosmetic purposes" is morally unacceptable. *The Cross and the Rain Forest*, pp. 118–19. Worth consulting also is the short essay by C. S. Lewis, "Vivisection," in *God in the Dock* (Grand Rapids: William B. Eerdmans, c. 1970), pp. 224–228.

Catechism and in Holy Scripture, if carefully followed, are able to bring about behavior that neither exploits and misuses animals and plants nor, on the other hand, that abdicates man's role as steward of creation. To desire to have as little effect on the natural life and environment of animals and plants, consistent with real human needs, is not to embrace a romantic attitude toward the natural world. Rather it is to remember that "by their mere existence" animals "bless [God] and give him glory" and that each of God's creations "reflects in its own way a ray of God's infinite wisdom and goodness." Every one of man's works must be in response to some genuine human need, or truly enhance the life of man, not just add useless gadgets or otherwise contribute to our fascination with what is new. A more sober use of created things would lead to an attitude more akin to the solidarity that we are to have with all creatures. It is a worthy effort of Catholics to promote such solidarity in order to change the often wasteful and profligate way that we live.

As I said previously, Satan promotes error in pairs, so that there will always be two warring camps, both zealously championing positions that are flawed, and both keenly aware of what is wrong with their opponent's point of view, but blind to what is wrong with their own. And in the modern world, too often Satan has managed to divide Catholics between two such camps. The only remedy, the only means by which we can escape this bitter but sterile secular warfare, is by obtaining an understanding of what the Church really teaches. Usually we will find that it coincides with neither of the two camps. And this is the case with the subject I have discussed here, our treatment of the environment. If we embrace what the Church teaches in Holy Scripture, in the Catechism and in other magisterial documents, then we can have some hope of avoiding being consigned to one of these two dreary secular camps. If we have some vision of the fullness of Catholic life and thought, then we can rejoice in our "solidarity [with] all creatures" at the same time as we recognize that we are the "summit of the Creator's work." Only thus can we ourselves contribute to the "beauty... order and harmony of the created world" and render it a more fitting gift to be placed at the feet of him, who is both "the image of the invisible God" and "the first-born of all creation" in whom "all things were created in heaven and on earth, visible and invisible," (Col. 1:15-16) and who one day will return to judge mankind and renew all things in himself.

6

Man and Cosmos

WHAT SCRIPTURE SHOWS US ABOUT THE DIGNITY OF ALL CREATION

CHRISTOPHER ZEHNDER

AMONG THE CLAIMS MADE AGAINST the Christian faith is that it is too dualistic, in the sense that it sets man in conflict against the natural world. The language of "fill the earth and subdue it" and of "dominion" over all other creatures (Gen. 1:28) suggests an adversarial relationship of conqueror and vanquished, or so some have claimed. The Christian faith has been accused of minimizing nature, reducing it to merely a fund of, albeit highly developed, raw material for exploitation.

Such claims ignore, of course, the nuances of such words as "dominion" and "subdue"—that dominion does not in itself equate with exploitation, and that even "subdue" need not imply a violent conquest. Of course, the story of Scripture is primarily about the drama of man's fall and God's salvation, not the natural world. Yet, an examination of Scripture will show that man's salvation includes more than man himself; even the non-human creation is implicated in it. Indeed, Scripture begins with the creation, not just of man, but of all things, the cosmos; and it ends not simply with the apotheosis of redeemed man but the renewal of all creation in a new heaven and a new earth. The cosmos and its creatures do not provide merely the shifting background scenery for the drama of salvation; they figure in the plot. Human salvation includes all that is man and of man—himself and the entire complex of reality of which he forms a part.

To see this we must begin at the beginning—the first chapter of Genesis.

79

At first sight, it may seem that Genesis presents creation as a series of discreet, extrinsically related events: God creates light and separates it from darkness; then, he moves on to the firmament, then the dry land, vegetation, the lights of heaven, aquatic creatures and birds, the living creatures of the land, and, at last man. Yet, a closer examination into Genesis suggests otherwise. Creation here is not a series of discreet events but, rather, a process of unfolding, a moving from the less perfect to the more perfect, from the good to (after the creation of man and woman) the "very good."

A cursory reading of the creation account might tempt us to predicate the "good" of the subhuman creatures and the "very good" separately of the being made in the image and likeness of God; yet, this is not the burden the words bear. God creates man and woman in his image, gives them dominion "over the fish of the sea and over the birds of the air and over every living thing that moves upon the earth." Still, it is only after God had completed his work that he, as it were, steps back and surveys *all* he has made, and pronounces judgment on the entire cosmos: "And God saw everything that he had made, and behold, it was very good" (Gen. 1:31).

It is not man, but the entire cosmos that is not just good but "very good." Of course, it is significant that this pronouncement is made only after man's creation, the completion and culmination of the creative acts that have gone before. Man is the crowning touch of God's art; he is that for the sake of which all things come to be. Nevertheless, Genesis here does not portray man as divided from or against all other creatures — as the very good from the merely good. It is rather the creation of man that confers on the whole of creation the property of its own excellence — its being "very good." That mankind can confer such a character of superlative goodness upon the whole of creation witnesses to a connection of man with everything else. Man, though transcending all lower creatures, is nevertheless with them a part of the cosmos. Only thus can they participate in his excellence.

Genesis thus outlines a natural order of priority among creatures that is not merely extrinsic; it is this order that forms the basis of the unity of the cosmos. In Genesis 1, we see that each stage of creation (first the inanimate, then the vegetative, then the locally motive and sensitive) raises the cosmos as a whole to a new level of perfection. The "it" that God sees as good on each day of creation is not just the creatures created on that day, but the whole earth. Yet, though at each stage of creation the whole cosmos is indeed good, it is not supremely good. Its very imperfection, as it were, yearns for a still higher perfection, its culmination in man. In himself, man is a microcosm of the whole, for he possesses each perfection of the lower creation: he can grow and develop physically, move himself about, and perceive the world through his senses. Yet, with all these, he has one perfection unique to himself—reason and free choice: the image of God. Without man, the universe reaches only to the level of sensitive life. Through man, it becomes "very good" by becoming noetic, by becoming aware of itself.

This is perhaps the inner meaning of the Garden of Eden. God does not place man in the garden merely to enjoy it; his task is to till it and keep it. As the primordial husbandman, Adam has the task of teasing out of creation an order of goodness of which it is *capax,* capable, but which it cannot attain without him. This is the meaning of his dominion, reflected in his naming of the animals. By naming them, man knows them; and by knowing them, he can rule them, becoming their master and lawgiver. By ruling them, he can bestow on them some share in the order of his own human reason.

Yet, in Genesis, man has another relationship—with God. Genesis speaks of God as walking in the Garden, of talking with man. In this way, man learns both what God commands and, to the degree he can, who God is. In the order of perfection man stands between God and all other material creatures and thus becomes the link of being between them. Man is like God, having an immaterial intellect and will; he takes part in the lower creation, through his body and senses. Man thus provides the bridge between the material and spiritual worlds. He is the *pontifex,* the bridge builder, the mediator between God and everything else.

This understanding perhaps sheds light on those curious passages of Scripture where beasts, plants, and even the inanimate forces of nature are exhorted to "bless the Lord" (Dan. 3:57-88) or "praise the Lord" (Ps. 148); that speak of mountains skipping like rams and hills like lambs (Ps. 113/114) before the majesty of God. We might be tempted to see such passages as anthropomorphic or instances of transferred epithet. Yet, if the cosmos is a unity comprising man and the subhuman creation; if it becomes, through man, noetic; if it is endowed with a superlative goodness through participation in man's perfection—why can it not, through man, share in the praise that man, as *pontifex*, offers up to God?

Man and every other creature praises God in another way—by attaining those goods which constitute their perfection. For man, this perfection lies ultimately in knowing God and loving him—the fulfillment of his nature as the image *and likeness* of God. While other creatures cannot be called images of God—rather, they are *vestigia* ("footprints," "tracks," "traces") of him—each according to its nature can share in a goodness that is analogous to the Good that is God. This perfection comes through the inner principle of each creature's own nature but it also rises out of the order with which man, as their lord, endows them. The more developed the perfection, the more perfect the analogy. The more perfect the analogy, the better each creature reflects God's goodness.

Thus we can say that all creatures in the cosmos share a common purpose—to reflect God. Though this purpose differs according to the mode of participation in God intrinsic to each being, extrinsically it stands as an end that binds all the diverse elements of the cosmos into one. The end of the universe is union with God—in man achieved explicitly in the union of his intellect and will with the divine essence, and in every other creature by a conforming to the perfection to which each of their natures tends. This end or purpose binds the cosmos together, endowing it with unity.

Of course, according to Scripture's account, Adam failed to be the *pontifex* of the fullness of cosmic unity. His disobedience thrust division between himself and his wife and between humanity and the created world—hence our so often shameful treatment of that very creation. The fruit of Adam's sin was death, both physical and spiritual, for him and his offspring. Yet, though Scripture does not dwell at length on the matter, Adam's fall had consequences for the natural, non-human world as well. Through the fall, creation "was subjected to futility," says St. Paul, it was cast into "bondage to decay." (See Rom. 8:18-25.) "We know," Paul says, "the whole creation has been groaning in travail together until now."

For St. Paul, creation's "groaning in travail" is not the expression of despair; it is more like the pains of a woman in childbirth. Indeed, earlier he calls it "eager longing" — "the creation," he says, "waits with eager longing for the revealing of the sons of God." From its "bondage to decay" it will be set free "and obtain the glorious liberty of the children of God." What is the "revealing of the sons of God" and "the glorious liberty of the children of God" but the restoration of man to paradise and his further exaltation to unity with God? St. Paul here teaches that this redemption and exaltation of man includes more than man. It implies the redemption and glorification of the cosmos.

St. Paul touches on this theme again in the hymn with which he opens his Epistle to the Ephesians: "Blessed be the God and Father of our Lord Jesus Christ, who has blessed us in Christ with every spiritual blessing in the heavenly places . . . " (Eph. 1:3-10). The hymn speaks of the mystery of Christ's redemption of man, predestined before the "foundation of the world." Through this redemption, God grants us forgiveness of sins, and we have the "riches of his grace . . . lavished upon us" through the revelation, "in all wisdom and insight," of the "mystery of his will according to his purpose which he set forth in Christ as a plan for the fulness of time." This plan, we learn, is of cosmic, not merely human, significance, for it is "to unite *all things* in him [Christ], things in heaven and things on earth." (Emphasis added.)

The Latin Vulgate has a somewhat different rendering of this hymn's peroration; it is, *instaurare omnia in Christo, quae in caelis at quae in terra sunt, in ipso* ("to renew all things in Christ, those which are in the heavens and those which are on the earth, in him.") Though the one version speaks of uniting and the other of renewing, the meanings are not mutually exclusive; for the process of redemption is a renewal of the original unity of man and creation, of man and cosmos. The renewal of man by a kind of necessity entails the renewal of *omnia*, "all things," for man is related to the universe (*universum*, "the entirety") as the head to a body, as a part to a whole.

In the Epistle to the Colossians (1:15-20), St. Paul uses similar language. There he speaks of Christ, in his divine nature, as the "first-born of all creation," through whom "all things were created, in heaven and on earth, visible and invisible." It is the divine Christ through whom "all things hold together" in unity. As man, Christ is the redeemer, "the head of the body, the church . . . the beginning, the first-born from the dead." The "fulness of God," St. Paul says, "was pleased to dwell" in him, "and through him to reconcile to himself all things, whether on earth or in heaven, making peace by the blood of his cross." The reconciliation here spoken of is not simply that of the Jews with the Gentiles in the unity of the Church, of which St. Paul speaks elsewhere; it is the reconciliation of *all things,* through the Church, in the unity of the cosmos.

Further, in his Epistle to the Philippians, St. Paul ties the resurrection of the body to this restoration of the cosmos:

> But our commonwealth is in heaven, and from it
> we await a Savior, the Lord Jesus Christ, who will
> change our lowly bodies to be like his glorious body,
> by the power which enables him even to subject all
> things to himself. (Phil. 3:20-21)

Again, the rendering of the Vulgate may help us to understand this passage:

> Nostra conversatio in caelis est, unde etiam sal-
> vatorem expectamus, Dominum nostrum Iesum
> Christum, qui reformabit corpus humilitatis nos-
> trae configuratum corpori claritatis suae secundum
> operationem qua possit etiam subicere sibi omnia.[1]

---

1 Our conversation is in the heavens, whence also we await a savior, our Lord Jesus Christ, who shall remake the body of our lowliness to be configured to the body of his glory according to the operation by which he would subject all things to himself.

The Apostle here seems to be saying that the change or remaking of our bodies—the resurrection of the flesh—proceeds by the same power or operation by which Christ subjects "all things" (*omnia*) to himself. In other words, the selfsame act of power that consummates man unites also the *universum,* the cosmos, in a common subjection to Christ.

Correlating these passages from St. Paul with what we have seen from Genesis, we may venture the following summary. Creation, though divided into seemingly discreet creative acts, is really one, albeit complex, act, culminating in the making of man. Far from being unrelated to other creatures, man is really their crown and perfection. His perfection is in a real way the universe's perfection, though not univocally throughout all levels of being. And man's fall entails the degradation of all things—and this because of their complex unity with man.

Yet, if the universe fell in man's fall, it rises with and through his renewal and resurrection. By becoming man, the New Adam, the Son of God takes on himself the priesthood that reconciles man with the cosmos, and both with God. He becomes the *pontifex,* the "bridgebuilder," that unifies the spiritual world with the material creation—and precisely by being man. Man's redemption is the universe's redemption by an inner necessity; for our perfection is the good to which the entire material universe strives. The whole cosmos participates in man's *theosis,* in man's becoming like God.

Thus, in a very real sense, man is brother to all creatures; every being is his kinsman—St. Francis of Assisi's "brother sun" and "sister moon"—and, even, "brother ass." They bear a likeness to what is in man, and though he transcends them, he shares in their perfections. Moreover, man's office (now in and through Christ) of *pontifex* demands a care, respect, and love for creatures that accords with their inherent goodness and dignity. For all creatures in and through man are destined to share in his own purpose and end: "the glorious liberty of the children of God."

7

The Numerical Pattern of the Cosmos and Divine Beauty in Christian Culture

DAVID CLAYTON

> Look how the floor of Heaven
> Is thick inlaid with patines of bright gold
> There's not the smallest orb that thou beholdest
> But in his motion like an angel sings
> Still quiring to the young-eyed cherubims
> Such harmony is in immortal souls
> — Lorenzo in Shakespeare, *Merchant of Venice*,
> Act V, scene 1

NUMBER CAN INDICATE QUALITY AS WELL AS QUANTITY

The natural order can be described mathematically. Long before the advent of modern science the ancients were aware of this, as they observed changes and movements of the constellations in the night sky. Ancient peoples (such as the Babylonians, Egyptians, Chinese, Indians, Greeks, Romans, Mayans, Incas, and Aztecs) observed these in great detail. Many, observing the connection between the pattern of motion of celestial bodies and the seasonal changes, thought that both were controlled by mysterious powers or gods. This is why, for example, the planets of the solar system that were visible to the naked eye bear the names, even to this day, of Roman gods.

For the first Christians, although recognizing that a single God controls all, the stars and the planets are still important. They became now signs of the rhythms of heaven to which the material world points.

For Catholics, of course, the focal point for the meeting of the material and the spiritual realms is in the liturgy — the formal worship of the Church. And all creation is now seen

87

to participate, in some way, in a liturgy of praise to God. The physical and the spiritual come together in a single point in the body and blood of Christ in the Eucharist. Everything else unfolds from this. Liturgy is not something that is confined to the services taking place in a church. Creation, through its being, is seen as giving liturgical praise to God.

As Erik Peterson wrote:

> The worship of the Church is not the liturgy of a human religious society, connected with a particular temple, but worship which pervades the whole universe and in which sun, moon, and all the stars take part.... The Church is no purely human religious society. The angels and saints in heaven belong to her as well. Seen in this light, the Church's worship is no merely human occasion. The angels and the entire universe take part in it.[1]

The Canticle of Daniel,[2] which is chanted regularly in the Divine Office, calls upon all of creation to bless the Lord, including the sun and moon, stars of the heavens, clouds of the sky, showers and rain, all animals and finally mankind. How, one might ask, can the conformity of the natural world to the patterns of heaven by those aspects of creation that can never know or love God be interpreted as giving praise to the Lord? This becomes clearer when we consider why God made creation. He made it so that through our perception of it, we might come to know him. Creation is made for us and we have a special place within it. The study of creation and how we perceive it can provide knowledge of its Creator. This knowledge is completed by God revealing the full truth to us himself, in the person of Christ. Creation speaks to us of the Creator in a way that is perceived at a deep, intuitive preconscious level when we recognize its beauty. When creation speaks to us in this way it 'gives praise' to the Lord. It is a praise that we are made to hear. As St Athanasius puts it: "Because an impress of Wisdom has been made in us and is

1 Erik Peterson, *The Angels and the Liturgy* (Herder & Herder, 1964), pp. 22, 50.
2 Daniel 3:57–88; and Divine Office: Lauds (Morning Prayer) of Sunday Week 1 and all Solemnities, Feasts and Memorials.

found in all the works of creation, it is natural that the true creative Wisdom should apply to itself what belongs to its impress, and say: 'The Lord created me in His work.'"[3] It is the underlying order of creation, the 'impress of Wisdom' that we recognize as beauty — cosmic beauty!

As a part of God's creation, albeit holding a special place, mankind and the angels give praise through their very existence too. But they have free will and have the additional capacity consciously to praise God, and to offer him thanksgiving through choice. This capacity is something that marks mankind out from all other earthly creatures, including other animate beings. In discerning how to harmonize his work of praise and gratitude to God — his liturgical activity — to that of heaven, man takes his cue, as it were, from the cosmos.

Christian cosmology is the study of the patterns and rhythms of the planets and the stars with the intention of ordering our work and praise to the work and praise of heaven, that is, the heavenly liturgy. The liturgical year of the Church is based upon these natural cycles. The date of Easter, for example, is calculated according to the phases of the moon. The purpose of earthly liturgy, and for that matter all Christian prayer, cannot be understood without grasping its harmony with the heavenly dynamic and the cosmos. The earthly liturgy should evoke a sense of the non-sensible aspect of the liturgy through its dignity and beauty. All our activities within it: kneeling, praying, standing, should be in accordance with the heavenly standard; the architecture of the church building, and the art and music used should all point us to what lies beyond it and give us a real sense that we are praising God with all of his creation and with the saints and angels in heaven. Pope Benedict XVI pointed to this dimension of Christian life in his book, *The Spirit of the Liturgy*. He discussed the importance of orienting church buildings and the Mass to the East, to face the rising sun, the symbol of the Risen One:

> The cosmic symbol of the rising sun expresses the universality of God above all particular places...

3 St Athanasius, Or 2, 78–79, taken from the Divine Office, Office of Readings, Week 30, Thursday.

But ... this turning toward the east also signifies that cosmos and saving history belong together. The cosmos is praying with us. It, too, is waiting for redemption. It is precisely this cosmic dimension that is essential to Christian liturgy. It is never performed solely in the self-made world of man. It is always a cosmic liturgy. The theme of creation is embedded in Christian prayer. It loses its grandeur when it forgets this connection.[4]

But why would we want to have a liturgical life at all? One reason is the desire of believers to worship him well by giving him our thanks and praise, as an end in itself simply because we love God. Another reason is that if we participate in the liturgy fully, it becomes an ordering principle for the whole of our lives; that is, by participating in an earthly liturgy that is in harmony with heaven, we receive grace that flows through our lives and overflows into the world. The liturgy is a portal that ushers the presence of God into our lives and (through our participation) the lives of others around us.

If we want to increase our collective ability to conform to grace, we should strive to make our participation in the liturgy conform to the pattern of heaven. The ceremonies of the Mass are gifts from God that can guide us so that we can love him more, and open us, and so the world, to grace. And number is an essential part of this, through the rhythmical repetitions of prayer and words, through posture, and in the production of beautiful music, art, and architecture that is "liturgical" even when it has a secular use.

THE PATTERNS OBSERVED IN THE COSMOS ARE DESCRIBED USING NUMBERS

The beauty of numbers is that once its significance has been discerned, that symbolism can be transferred, so to speak, and applied to any aspect of our lives through the ordering of time, space, art, and music in accordance with it. This is its special mystery. When we apply the liturgical numbers of the cosmos to the rhythms and actions of our lives extending beyond that

4 Joseph Cardinal Ratzinger, *The Spirit of the Liturgy* (Ignatius Press, 2000), pp. 70, 76.

part lived in the church building, the whole of life becomes infused with a liturgical rhythm. We can imbue all our activities and work with a heavenly grace and beauty if the application of this symbolism is appropriate to that to which it is applied. All aspects of the cosmos in the broadest sense can come under consideration here. It is not simply the pattern of the motion of the planets that is an object of study; we can look at the proportions of man and his work, including the mathematical patterns that describe harmony in instrumental music.

In our consideration of the symbolic meaning of number, it is important to understand that number is not a cause of the property it symbolizes. In his commentary on the Creation story of Genesis,[5] Benedict XVI describes how the number 10 in the Old Testament symbolizes the authority of God. So we recognize that there are 10 commandments, and also that in the creation process the phrase 'God said.' appears 10 times. The pattern of 10 applied to commands from God connects the two together and simultaneously reflects something that is true about them. I cannot however lend the authority of God to something that does not have it simply by attaching the number 10 to it in some way. If I say, 'Give me $1,000,' for example, it does not suddenly become the will of God as I utter the tenth repetition of the phrase. That would be a false symbolism.

The writers of Scripture used this special property of number, that of being easily transferred from one entity or idea, regularly to connect different events, so affecting our understanding of each. For example, according to another traditional interpretation of the gospels, when Christ commanded the distribution of food to feed the 5,000, there was a surplus which was gathered up in 12 baskets. Early commentators, such as Origen,[6] thought that the number twelve indicated the 12 tribes of Israel and the superabundant and spiritual nourishment that Christ was bringing them. Similarly, after the feeding of the 4,000 there were seven baskets left. Seven was the number of the gentile tribes who were displaced from the Promised, and so this

5 Cardinal Joseph Ratzinger: *In the Beginning: A Catholic Understanding of the Story of Creation and the Fall* (Grand Rapids: William B. Eerdsmans, 1995).
6 Origen, *Commentary on the Gospel of Matthew*, bk. XI, 20

indicates now that Christ has come to give everlasting life to all peoples, Israelite (12) and Gentile (7) alike. There are eight nations in all therefore, symbolizing all people, who comprise the mystical body of Christ who is, symbolically, the eighth day.

Seven and its completion in eight often occur together. Seven also symbolizes the number of the old covenant coming from the seven days of creation and the connected pattern of living according to seven days in the week. (Incidentally, this associates the seven days of the week with the seven planets visible to the naked eye, and even today Romance languages such as French for example, use the Latin names for those planets.) Eight symbolizes the new covenant, because Christ ushers in the new order through his life, death and resurrection. We celebrate that resurrection on Sunday (day of both the sun and the Son), which is simultaneously the eighth day of the previous week, and the first of the next.

This pattern of (7 + 1) governs much of the structure of Christian liturgy and prayer connecting each to the realization that the fulfillment of the old covenant is in Christ, who is the new covenant, and whom we encounter most profoundly in our worship in the Eucharist.

We see this pattern elsewhere in the liturgy. Aside from the weekly cycle it governs the daily cycle of prayer too. In the sixth century St Benedict, the founder of the Benedictine Order, underlined an aspect of "liturgical number" in chapter 16 of his Rule by looking to the Old Testament: "the prophet says: 'Seven times daily I have sung your praises'" [Ps. 119:164 and Psalm 118/119:62] "At midnight I rise to praise you." He then tells us we will 'cleave to this sacred number' by singing the psalms eight times a day at Matins, Lauds, Prime, Tierce, Sext, None, Vespers, and Compline.

Man cannot address his attention to prayer constantly, but must attend to the needs of life. These eight occasions of prayer during the day are portals through which grace pours into daily life and to the degree we cooperate, sanctifies the times between prayer by integrating them with the cosmic rhythm of the liturgy. Even if we do not participate in all offices ourselves, the Church collectively does and we benefit from the prayers of those who pray on behalf of the Church.

To give another example, there are seven petitions in the Lord's Prayer. The first three relate to heavenly things, the last three to earthly things and the central petition, the fourth is 'Give us this day our daily bread'. As St. Thomas Aquinas explains in his commentary,[7] this petition can be understood in two ways: First it is "the sacramental Bread, the daily use of which is profitable to man, and in which all the other sacraments are contained, or of the bread of the body, so that it denotes all sufficiency of food." So again we see a 7+1 structure. This is indeed, therefore, the Lord's prayer, indicated by the fact that he gave it to us, and that its content and place within the liturgy speak of him, but also by the numerical pattern in which the text is constructed.

Those who are aware of the symbolism of numbers will very likely recognize it and then delight in the idea that the structure and information that texts contain is ordered according to the same pattern of the cosmos, and that both conform to the pattern of heaven.

The assumption of the ancients was that we are made by God to see his mark in both the material and spiritual order and so delight in a pattern that directs us to divine beauty. While understanding the nature of pattern can give us greater sensitivity to its beauty, it is not absolutely necessary. We do not need to know anything about the mathematics of harmony and proportion in order to respond to the beauty of the cosmos. Similarly, we can respond to the beauty of the Lord's prayer without knowing that the thematic structural symmetry is governed by the numbers seven and eight.

Artists, writers and architects can choose to incorporate this symbolism into their work so as to enhance its attraction, if done appropriately, and reveal truth. Raphael, for example, working in 16th century Italy, in the octagonal design of his 'Mond' conveys the significance of the 'eighth day' symbolizing the incarnation, life, death and resurrection of Christ. One can see the octagon traced out by the heads of the onlookers below and the heads and feet of the two flanking angels. This is not intended simply to be a coded language that the cognoscenti can see.

7 *Summa Theologiae*, II-II, q. 83, art. 9.

Rather, the expectation is that when the design of the painting is in harmony with the truths the artist intends to portray, then it will sensitize our hearts to the reception of that truth and will appeal to us at a deep, intuitive level as an object of beauty. The same logic underlies the convention of octagonal design of baptismal fonts and baptistries and the octagonal patterns in the floor tiles of central aisles of churches.

WHERE CAN WE SEE SYMBOLIC NUMBERS?

There are three fundamental sources of significance in number:

1. Revelation through Scripture;
2. Observation of any aspect of the natural world, which includes planetary motion, the proportions of man, and the patterns of harmony in instrumental music, which is caused by the motion of matter;
3. Consideration of numbers significant in the abstracted world of mathematics.

Using these three sources man can employ this symbolism in his work as an authentic aspect of Christian culture. Traditional Christian culture becomes, therefore, for modern man who is for most part detached from it, a fourth potential source for us to see the symbolic use of numbers.

Though not dealt with in depth here, there is another aspect of the symbolism of number that is important, and that is number in relation. Certain combinations of numbers have significance too, and these combinations are discerned from the same sources as above. This is called 'harmonious proportion'.

The second and third items listed above are Christian traditions that stem originally from ancient Greece and the philosopher Pythagoras[8]; but are nevertheless consistent with the principles given in Scripture.

Pope Benedict XVI discusses the mathematical ordering of time, space and matter in his book *The Spirit of the Liturgy*.

---

8 By tradition Pythagoras lived around 550 BC. His ideas were conveyed largely through the works of Plato, especially the *Timaeus*; and through those of Aristotle in works now lost but referred to by later writers, such as Boethius.

An extended quotation from this work is justified, in order to sum up what has been said so far:

> Among the Fathers, it was especially St Augustine who tried to connect this characteristic view of the Christian liturgy with the world view of Greco-Roman antiquity. In his early work 'On Music' he is still completely dependent on the Pythagorean theory of music. According to Pythagoras the cosmos was constructed mathematically, a great edifice of numbers. Modern physics, beginning with Kepler, Galileo and Newton, has gone back to this vision and, through the mathematical interpretation of the universe, has made possible the technological use of its powers. For the Pythagoreans, this mathematical order of the universe ('cosmos' means 'order'!) was identical with the essence of beauty itself. Beauty comes from meaningful inner order. And for them this beauty was not only optical but also musical. Goethe alludes to this idea when he speaks of the singing contest of the fraternity of the spheres: the mathematical order of the planets and their revolutions contains a secret timbre, which is the primal form of music. The courses of the revolving planets are like melodies, the numerical order is the rhythm, and the concurrence of the individual courses is the harmony. The music made by man must, according to this view, be taken from the inner music and order of the universe, be inserted into the 'fraternal song' of the 'fraternity of the spheres'. The beauty of music depends on its conformity to the rhythmic and harmonic laws of the universe. The more that human music adapts itself to the musical laws of the universe, the more beautiful it will be.
>
> St Augustine first took up this theory and then deepened it. In the course of history, transplanting it into the worldview of faith was bound to bring with it a twofold personalization. Even the Pythagoreans did not interpret the mathematics of the universe in an entirely abstract way. In the view of the ancients, intelligent actions presupposed an intelligence that caused them. The intelligent,

mathematical movements of the heavenly bodies were not explained, therefore, in a purely mechanical way; they could only be understood on the assumption that the heavenly bodies were animated, and were themselves 'intelligent'. For Christians, there was a spontaneous turn at this point from the stellar deities to the choirs of angels that surround God and illumine the universe. Perceiving the 'music of the cosmos' thus becomes listening to the song of angels, and the reference to Isaiah chapter 6 ('Holy, holy, holy is the LORD of hosts; the whole earth is full of his glory.' Isaiah 6:1-3) naturally suggests itself.

But a further step was taken with the help of the Trinitarian faith, faith in the Father, the Logos, and the Pneuma. The mathematics of the universe does not exist by itself, nor, as people now came to see, can it be explained by stellar deities. It has a deeper foundation: the mind of the Creator. It comes from the Logos, in whom, so to speak, the archetypes of the world's order are contained. The Logos, through the Spirit, fashions the material world according to these archetypes. In virtue of his work in creation, the Logos is, therefore, called the 'art of God' (ars = techne!). The Logos himself is the great artist, in whom all works of the art — the beauty of the universe — have their origin. To sing with the universe means, then, to follow the track of the Logos and to come close to him. All true human art is an assimilation to the artist, to Christ, to the mind of the Creator. The idea of the music of the cosmos, of singing with angels, leads back again to the relation of art to logos, but now it is broadened and deepened in the context of the cosmos. Yes, it is the cosmic context that gives art in the liturgy both its measure and its scope. A merely subjective 'creativity' is no match for the vast compass of the cosmos and for the message of beauty. When a man conforms to the measure of the universe, his freedom is not diminished but expanded to a new horizon.[9]

9 Joseph Cardinal Ratzinger, *The Spirit of the Liturgy* (Ignatius Press, 2000), pp. 152–4.

THE BEAUTY OF THE COSMOS & THE BEAUTY OF GOD

An artist who seeks to tap into a creativity that draws on the "vast compass of the cosmos and for the message of beauty" could do well to take this last point to heart. It is hard to see how any artist can truly reunite his art with the principle of liturgical number and ultimately all beauty if he is not himself living a life infused with liturgical rhythm. Abbot Suger, who built St Denis, the first gothic church, in France in the 12th century, wrote as much when he described the process of the design and creation of the building. He drew on the theology of Dionysius the Areopagite as received through the works of John Scotus Erigena and Maximus the Confessor. As Otto von Simson wrote, Suger believed that "the mystical vision of harmony can become an ordering principle for the artist only if it has first taken possession of his soul and become the ordering principle of all its faculties and aspiration... To Suger, as to his master St Augustine, this process is not so much the physical labour as it is the gradual edification of those who take part in the building, the illumination of their souls by the vision of divine harmony that is then reflected in the material work of art."[10]

For Catholics, this process of personal re-ordering by prayer starts with the Mass and the Divine Office. From that foundation in Christ, we may begin to integrate all the other aspects of life. Underlying this argument is the assumption that the cosmos is beautiful, and the beauty that it possesses points to an even purer beauty, the heavenly beauty and ultimately to Beauty itself, God.

The Church Father who is credited, along with Augustine, with bringing these ideas into Christian thought is a Catholic martyr, canonized as St Severinus Boethius, but usually known simply as Boethius. Pope Benedict XVI made a special point of drawing our attention to Boethius in a general audience in Rome on 12 March 2008.

Boethius was born in Rome in about 480. Recognized as a brilliant scholar at an early age, he wrote manuals on arithmetic, geometry, music and astronomy, four of the seven liberal arts,

10   Otto von Simson, *The Gothic Cathedral* (Harper and Row, NY, 1964), p. 126

called collectively the 'quadrivium'. The manual on arithmetic and part of that on music survive. He used the categories of Greek philosophy to present the Christian faith, seeking a synthesis between the Hellenistic-Roman heritage and the Gospel message. Boethius has been described as the last representative of ancient Roman culture and the first of the Medieval intellectuals. His most famous work is *De Consolatione Philosophiae*, (*The Consolation of Philosophy*). It was written while in prison at the hands of the Ostrogothic King, Theodoric. In this work he draws extensively, though not exclusively, on the philosophy behind the quadrivium. His insight in applying the lessons of the study of something as abstract as arithmetic to the practical considerations of life — and adversity that, please God, few of us will have to face — can only be marveled at. Boethius was executed on 23 October 524. The date of his martyrdom is commemorated as his feast.

The influence of Boethius's work lasted well beyond his life. For example, these works are seminal in the rise of the 12th-century schools, especially that of Chartres. Dante, who structured his work according to numerical symbolism, read him[11]; Geoffrey Chaucer translated his work into Middle English and thereafter he structured his literary works, for example, *Troilus and Creseyde* and *The Knight's Tale* (from *The Canterbury Tales*)[12], around the ideas that Boethius had proposed. C. S. Lewis wrote that the *Consolation* "was for centuries one of the most influential books ever written in Latin."[13] It has recently been proposed, and broadly accepted, that a unifying principle of Lewis's seven chronicles of Narnia is a Christian cosmology of the sort that Boethius uses.[14]

The reason for incorporating a Christian cosmology in these works is deeper than a superficial desire to conform to an ancient symbolism that only a few will recognize. The assumption is that human beings are hardwired to pick up

11   Henry Chadwick, *Boethius: The Consolations of Music, Logic, Theology and Philosophy* (Oxford: Clarendon Press, 1990), pp. 223, 252.

12   *Consolation of Philosophy*, in introductory notes by P. G. Walsh (Oxford University, 1999), p. xlvii.

13   *The Discarded Image* (Cambridge, 1971) p. 75.

14   Michael Ward, *Planet Narnia: The Seven Heavens in the Imagination of C. S. Lewis* (Oxford University, 2008)

information presented in accordance with the pattern of the divine mind. Nature appears beautiful because we recognize in it the thumbprint of the Creator. When the work of man is structured in the same way, we see the mark of inspiration from the Creator and we are drawn to it. This can be at different levels. If the dimensions of the page of a book, and the print within it conform to these proportions, then the eye finds it easier to take in the information. If the dramatic structure of the story being told within it also conforms to this divine model, then the author can decide to place those moments of high drama within the structure in such a way that they will have an even greater impact than the narrative alone would give.

For both Augustine and Boethius, number and due proportion hold a special key to the order of heaven and ultimately the 'mind of the Creator'. Mathematics might be described as the science of pattern. As already mentioned, philosophically it is seen as a stepping stone that leads the mind to contemplation of the spiritual because it can be considered as a descriptor of the material world, and can be conceived in the abstract without application to physical quantities in its own 'world' of mathematics. Modern science makes use of its power to quantify. The ancients saw this too, but they took it further. They equated sensible beauty (that is beauty as perceived through the senses) with the symmetry and harmony of relationships in the non-sensible mathematical world. So for the ancients a beautiful harmony in music reflected a harmonious mathematical relationship (derived from the consideration of the relative lengths of string that produced the notes when plucked).

NUMBER REFLECTING HIERARCHY IN CREATION

Many modern mathematicians see a beauty in the form of a perfect mathematical solution to a problem regardless of whether or not it has a material application. But the Church Fathers saw in this a hierarchy, consistent with the hierarchy of God's creation. The more perfect the symmetry or harmony in the relationship, the more beautiful. So this gave rise to special regard to certain numbers and certain mathematical relationships. This was confirmed for them by the fact that the writers of the Bible consistently highlight the number of days, the dimensions of buildings, the number of repetitions of acts. As God's revelation, the Bible can be considered an independent and authoritative source of significant numbers. These 'governing' numbers could be used to classify and order the observed patterns in the universe. Indeed, the view was taken that the Bible could not be interpreted properly without knowledge of the hierarchical nature of numbers. St. Augustine wrote:

> An unfamiliarity with numbers makes unintelligible many things that are said figuratively and mystically in scripture. An intelligent intellect, if I may put it thus, cannot fail to be intrigued by the meaning of the fact that Moses and Elijah and the Lord himself fasted 40 days. The knotty problem of the figurative significance of this event cannot be solved except by understanding and considering the number, which is four times 10, and signifies the knowledge of all things woven into the temporal order. The courses of the day and the year are based on the number four: the day is divided into the hours of morning, afternoon, evening and night; the year into months of the spring, summer, autumn and winter. While we live in the temporal order, we must fast and abstain from the enjoyment of what is temporal for the sake of eternity in which we desire to live, but it is actually the passage of time by which the lesson of despising the temporal and seeking the eternal is brought home to us. Then the number 10 signifies the knowledge of the Creator and creation: the Trinity is the number of the Creator, while the number seven symbolises the creation because it represents life and the body. The former has three elements (hence the precept that God must be loved with the whole heart, the whole soul, and the whole mind [Matt. 22:37] and as for the body, the four elements of which it consists are perfectly obvious [Fire, earth, water, air]. To live soberly according to the significance of number 10 — conveyed to us temporally (hence multiplied by the number four) — and abstain from the pleasures

of the world; this is the significance of the 40-day fast. This is enjoined by the law, as represented by Moses; by prophecy, as represented by Elijah; and by the Lord himself, who to symbolize that he enjoyed the testimony of law and the prophets, shone out in the midst of them on the mountain as the three amazed disciples looked on. [Matt. 17:1-8; Mark 9:2-6][15]

Even though Augustine describes at length the root of the significance of 40 in the 40-day fast, this passage of his will still be unclear to many, for he assumes an acquaintance with the basic ideas of significant numbers beyond that of most modern readers.

As an example of how the interrelationships of numbers within the abstract world of mathematics can be significant, consider the number six. Six has significance in arithmetic because it is a 'perfect number'. A perfect number is one that is numerically equal to the sum of its aliquot parts. The aliquots of six are those numbers that can be multiplied by a whole number to give six. So the aliquot parts of six are 1, 2 and 3. Six is perfect because it is the sum of 1, 2 and 3. It has a higher degree of perfection in that it is also the product of 1, 2 and 3. It is both the product and the sum of its aliquot parts. The number six has biblical significance also because the work of creation was carried out in six working days. St. Augustine notes the connection between the two and sees the arithmetic principle as the governing principle. In the *City of God* he says: "Six is a number that is perfect in itself, and not because God created the world in six days: rather the contrary is true. God created the world in six days because this number is perfect, and it would remain perfect, even if the work of the six days did not exist."[16] The application of this understanding is the ordering of human time into seven-day weeks, with one day of rest, mirroring the work pattern of God in creation.

15 *De Doctrina Christiana*, bk. II, XVI, 24–25.
16 *De Civitate Dei*, bk. XI, Ch. 30, "Of the perfection of the number six, which is the first of the numbers which is composed of its aliquot parts."

BEAUTY AND LOVE

There is an even deeper meaning of that 'meaningful inner order' referred to by Pope Benedict XVI. For the Christian it is Love, that is God. The poem in Book 2 of Boethius's *Consolation of Philosophy* is worth quoting. It describes how this ordering principle of harmony of both heaven and earth can be identified with the ordering principle of harmonious human relationships, pure love — 'Love' — that is God:

> Why does the world with steadfast faith
> Harmonious changes put in train?
> Why do the ever warring seeds
> Eternal treaties yet maintain?
>
> Why does the sun in golden car
> Inaugurate the rose-red day?
> Appoint the moon to rule the night
> Once Hesperous[17] has led the way?
>
> And greedy sea confine its waves
> Within the boundaries it has set
> Forbidding the encroaching lands
> Extend the coastline further yet?
>
> The power that contains this chain
> Of natures orderings is Love.
> Love governs lands and seas alike
> Love orders to the heavens above.
>
> Should Love once slacken tight its rein
> And cease to order near and far
> The mutual love which all things show
> Will in a moment turn to war.
>
> With beauteous motions Nature's parts
> In fond compact invigorate
> The fabric of the universe
> Which else they'd strive to dissipate.

17 Hesperous is the Evening Star and Morning Star, Venus. In Christian cosmology, Venus is the symbol of the Mother of God as transferred from the Roman goddess for whom the planet is named.

Such love embraces nations too;
In hallowed pacts it them combines
With chaste affections man and wife
In solemn wedlock it entwines.

Love's laws most trusty comrades bind
How happy is the human race,
If Love by which the heavens are ruled,
To rule men's minds is set in place![18]

When we apprehend beauty, it stirs in us that which causes us to love. When they spoke of love, the Fathers were not referring so much to a feeling or emotion (although these are not unconnected), as to the inclination to act in relation to others. A true loving relationship is simultaneously one of properly ordered and mutual self-sacrifice, properly ordered dynamic of gift to and reception from the other (referred to by Benedict XVI as *agape* and *eros*[19]).

Human love has no power or meaning if it is not intimately connected with our love for God and, more importantly, his love for us. God's love for us is already there, constant and unmoving. With us it is not so much a question of whether or not we love. We all do. It is more a question of what we love. Do we love what is good, or what is not good; or as St. Augustine put it, what is God, or what is not God? When mankind loves well, he exercises his free will in harmony with God's will and his love is in accord with God's. The resulting loving action is graceful and the work it produces is beautiful.

MORAL AND SPIRITUAL BEAUTY
REFLECTS THE SAME ORDER

The principle of beauty relates as much to abstract principles of truth as it does to the proportions of a beautiful building. This leads to the idea that a good life is also a beautiful life because of its possession of spiritual and moral beauty. The abstract world of arithmetic is seen as a stepping stone for the mind in its contemplation and grasping of morality. The

18 Boethius, *The Consolation of Philosophy*, translated by P. G. Walsh. (Oxford University, 2000), pp. 38–9.
19 *Deus caritas est*, no. 3.

mind that is formed, through a good education, in the symmetry and beauty of numbers, is more likely to reach instinctively for objective moral truth because it will be attracted by its beauty. St. Thomas Aquinas stated that three qualities are required for beauty:

> In the first place integrity or perfection, since incomplete things, precisely because they are such, are deformed; due proportion and harmony among parts is also required; finally clarity or splendour [claritas].[20]

'Integrity' or 'perfection' relates the form of something to its intended purpose. One might refer to this as a kind of harmony also — the harmony between what an object is and the original idea, conceived in the creative intellect, of what it ought to be. Since the Fall, the order that pervaded the material universe has been ruptured so that it is no longer perfect. This has created disorder — there is no order outside the divine order — and in a fallen world the correspondence to the divine order has diminished.

Ugliness appears where there is disorder. Just as disorder is not a thing in itself, but the absence of order; ugliness is not a thing in itself, but a lack of perfection in regard to beauty. In general, however, we would say that although the universe is not perfect, and not as beautiful as when redeemed at the final judgement, it is still good and still beautiful, but also it points to the ideal of what it ought to be and what it will be in the restored Eden.

Claritas is the means by which the harmony and integrity of the object become graspable, that is knowable, by our intellects. When something is beautiful, it 'speaks' to us of its harmonious nature. During this life, beautiful things usually 'speak' to us for the most part through interaction with the senses. *Claritas* is often equated with a literal splendour of bright light, or bright color. Aquinas himself used this example to illustrate the point and said that we describe things whose colors are clear and brilliant as beautiful. However, something can be beautiful in concept, even if its interaction with the senses is

20 *Summa Theologiae*, I, q. 39, art. 8

not literally dazzling—we can be attracted to the beauty of an idea of something described in writing, even if written in a dull, moth-eaten book. Also we can perceive a moral beauty in the actions of a good man. Perhaps even a man whom we have not met or seen, but simply have been told about by another. When we are told of the lives of the saints, their action possesses harmony with the will of God and has *claritas*, a brilliance that communicates itself to us. We grasp through the relating of the story that the abstract principles of morality revealed in their actions relate to the standards of goodness and truth that we know. St. Thomas again, "Spiritual beauty consists in the fact that the conduct and the deeds of a person are well proportioned in accordance with the light of reason."[21]

As already mentioned, *claritas* includes conventional optical light, but can also be equated with the 'uncreated' light that is described as shining from the transfigured Christ and in the book of Revelation as illuminating heaven for Saint John in his vision, and for us also, if we reach that heavenly state. All of creation exists for us to know. And each harmonious form that exists has its own divinely orchestrated package of 'claritas' that characterizes its unique beauty and makes the truth of what it is knowable and communicable to our minds. If we are ever united with God in heaven then we will know all beauty fully.

> Hence it happens that this universal architecture of the world is an exceedingly great light made up of many parts and many lights to reveal the pure species of intelligible things and to intuit them with the mind's eye, as divine grace and the help of the reason work together in the heart of the wise believer. When theologians call God the father of Lights they do well, because from him come all things, through which and in which He manifests himself and in the light of His wisdom they are unified and made.[22]

Spiritual beauty is assumed to possess harmony and due proportion, very often perceived intuitively. Virtue, for example, speaks to us of its goodness even if we have never been

21 *Summa Theologiae*, II-II, q. 145, art. 2
22 John Scotus Erigena, *Commentary on the Celestial Hierarchy* [of Dionysius the Pseudo-Areopagite], 1.

taught that there are seven cardinal virtues. And due proportion always, in principle, relates to a numerical description.

> Since, therefore, all things are beautiful and to some
> measure pleasing; and [since] there is no Beauty and
> pleasure without proportion, and proportion is to
> be found primarily in numbers; all things must have
> numerical proportion. Consequently "number is
> the principal exemplar in the mind of the Creator"
> and as such it is the principal trace that, in things,
> leads to wisdom. Since this trace is extremely clear
> to all and is closest to God, it leads us to Him...[23]

BEAUTY, GOD'S CALL THAT LEADS US TO HAPPINESS

For Boethius writing in his *Consolation*, the desire for
happiness is equated exactly with desire for unity with God,
when we partake of the divine nature in heaven. The division between heaven and earth is not a chasm between two
geographical places that can only be crossed at death; but
rather a continuum between two different modes of existence.
We can experience the heavenly, divine state here on earth
and all of us do by degrees when we are happy. God, he
says (reproducing the argument used by other Fathers) is the
highest good that can be imagined. He then says that perfect
happiness is the highest good that men seek and therefore
God is happiness. He continues:

> Since men become happy by achieving happi-
> ness and happiness itself is divinity, clearly they
> become happy by attaining divinity. Now just as
> men become just by acquiring justice, and wise by
> acquiring wisdom, so by the same argument they
> must become gods by acquiring divinity. Hence
> every happy person is God: God is by nature one
> only, but nothing prevents the greatest possible
> number from sharing in that divinity.[24]

Later he equates this good that we all seek with Love, the
source of our life and our final end.

---

23 St Bonaventure, *Itinerarium Mentis in Deum*, bk. II,10.
24 Boethius, *Consolation of Philosophy*, bk. III, 10, p. 59.

Love is that common fount of all
All seek adhesion to that end, the good.
Things cannot otherwise survive
Unless in Love's renewed embrace, they flow
Back to the source, their fount of Life.[25]

This reveals the reason for our wishing to conform our lives and our work with the underlying harmony of heaven as revealed in the traditional discipline of arithmetic and applied in all aspects of our lives. In doing so we have joy in our lives and create an environment that tends to influence others to accept that joy too.

For all Christians happiness is achieved by the possession of the Good, God. God has already given himself to us. If we wish to accept that gift we strive to follow God's will. The life of beauty is one infused with and revealing harmonious relationships that reflect the divine order. Furthermore, the beautiful life is a happy life. It is this beauty, as a sign of the possession of joy, that draws others to us and then to the source of that joy, God.

I shall give the last word to Pope Benedict XVI, in his address at Bagnoregio, Italy on September 6, 2009. Speaking of St. Bonaventure he said:

> In addition to being a seeker of God, St. Bonaventure was a seraphic singer of creation who, following St. Francis, learned to "praise God in all and through all creatures," in which "shines the omnipotence, wisdom and goodness of the Creator."[26] St. Bonaventure presents a positive vision of the world, gift of God's love to men: He recognizes in it the reflection of the highest Goodness and Beauty that, following St. Augustine and St. Francis, assures us that it is God himself. God has given it all to us. From him, as original source, flow truth, goodness and beauty. To God, as on the steps of a stairway, one ascends until arriving and almost attaining the highest Good and in him we find our joy and peace.

25 Boethius, *Consolation*, bk. IV, 6, p. 94.
26 Bonaventure, *Itinerarium Mentis in Deum*, bk. I, 10

How useful it would be if also today we rediscovered the beauty and value of creation in the light of divine goodness and beauty! In Christ, observed St. Bonaventure, the universe itself can again be the voice that speaks of God and leads us to explore his presence; exhorts us to honour and glorify him in everything. Herein we perceive the spirit of St. Francis, with whom our saint shared love for all creatures.

8

Genetically Modified Organisms
A CATHOLIC'S
ANIMADVERSIONS

PETER A. KWASNIEWSKI

C LONING AND SOME OTHER EXPERI-
mental or therapeutic procedures that constitute a
direct assault on the human person's dignity have
been condemned by the Church's Magisterium, but the case
is not so clear with the genetic engineering of organisms
more broadly speaking. In St. John Paul II's discourse for
the 35th Assembly of the Worldwide Medical Association in
1983, we read that certain genetic manipulations violate the
person's rightful autonomy by reducing a human life to an
object.[1] One could ask, more broadly: even if no non-human
organism has the kind of inherent rights that distinguish
persons from non-persons, should *any* natural thing ever be
reduced to the status of a mere object? In his message for
the World Day of Peace on 1st January 1990, the John Paul
said the following:

> We can only look with deep concern at the enor-
> mous possibilities of biological research. We are not
> yet in a position to assess the biological disturbance
> that could result from indiscriminate genetic manip-
> ulation and from the unscrupulous development of
> new forms of plant and animal life, to say nothing
> of unacceptable experimentation regarding the ori-
> gins of human life itself. It is evident to all that in
> any area as delicate as this, indifference to funda-
> mental ethical norms, or their rejection, would lead
> mankind to the very threshold of self-destruction.

[1] The discourse, given in French, is contained in *Insegnamenti di Giovanni Paolo II,* vol. VI, 2 (July–December 1983), pp. 917–23.

In an address to participants at a convention in 1982 on biological experimentation sponsored by the Pontifical Academy of Sciences, Pope John Paul did not directly engage the question of the licitness and prudence of gene modification, but seemed to take for granted the licitness of at least some procedures, repeating that research and application must be governed by universal moral norms (which are, to a large extent, left unspecified in this address). An endorsement of genetically modified organisms [GMOs] is implicit in the statement: "I wish to recall . . . the important advantages that come from *the increase of food products* and from the formation of new vegetal species for the benefit of all, especially people most in need."²

The procedure's moral permissibility would appear to be upheld by the Magisterium, if we may regard as signs the amount of favorable discussion that has taken place under the auspices of the Vatican, as well as the largely optimistic treatment found in the *Compendium of the Social Doctrine of the Church* (nn. 472–480).³

However, the debate is not exhausted by settling the question of licitness. It is one thing to decide on the simple morality of GMOs — that is, whether or not fashioning such things is *per se* immoral — and another to make a prudential decision about the wisdom of their development, usage, and multiplication. A perusal of the relevant Vatican documentation indicates how carefully endorsements are hedged about with cautionary notes and conditions.⁴ As always, if Church officials take a stance in regard to a strictly prudential matter such as the *use* of GMOs, they do so as offering their personal opinion — based, undoubtedly, on some legitimate reasons, but not binding on Catholics who evaluate the concrete situation differently. The non-sinfulness of a given technology does not entail the desirability of its deployment. For example, if a new technology would allow a cost-effective substitution

---

2   The text, in English, may be found in *Insegnamenti di Giovanni Paolo II,* vol. V, 3 (July–December 1982), pp. 889–93, n. 6, emphasis in original.

3   It cannot be overlooked that the vagueness and ambivalence of most of the official statements to date render a clear-cut stance, whether for or against, hard to maintain. I have begun to wonder if this is not an unintentional admission on the part of the people who write these documents that the problem is too complicated for them, and that they would prefer not to get too involved in the business of discernment and judgment. If so, it may be that such statements are ultimately more a disservice than a service to people who are actually attempting such discernment and judgment.

4   For example, the *Compendium of Social Doctrine* states that man is permitted to intervene to improve characteristics or properties of living beings, but then says that any intervention that may have a forceful and widespread impact on organisms should not be enacted lightly or irresponsibly (no. 473). But what does this mean, concretely? If genetic modification is not an example of a procedure with deep, far-reaching, and worrisome implications for the environment, what is?

of computers for bus drivers and train engineers, one could still doubt the wisdom of wiping out thousands of jobs that bring wages to workers and put a human face on an otherwise impersonal system. I will come back later to this modern temptation of doing certain things mainly because we have figured out how to do them. We exult in our triumphant dominion, but often fail to ask probing and uncomfortable questions about the potential dark side of our triumph.

We can sum up in three points what has been said so far about magisterial interventions. First, it is one thing for the Holy Father to address a question with an explicit intention to determine the answer for all Catholics, and another thing for him to speak of some matter in a more hypothetical vein, offering his own judgment.[5] This latter ought to be taken seriously, but it does not yet amount to definitive teaching.

Second, if the pope were to state that a particular form of technology (such as GMOs) is a positive benefit and should be deployed on a wide scale, this could *only* be a prudential judgment on his part, not a doctrinal one; the pope has no competency to select, much less command the use of, secular means for secular ends (though clearly he may forbid Catholics to use any morally dubious or disordered means, whether directed to good or to bad ends). Put differently, for the use of GMOs to be *obligatory,* it would have to be proved that *only* by their use could poverty or food shortages be solved. Even the most vigorous promoter of GMOs would not honestly be able to assert this, since in contingent human affairs there are many possible solutions, and it is often better morally to adopt a materially less satisfactory solution.[6]

Third, what a Congregation or a Council or a particular curial official declares cannot be taken as the Holy See's or Holy Father's position; much less can it be taken as a definitive

5 The papal intention is clear from such circumstances as the manner of speaking, the type of document employed, and the frequency of a doctrine's reiteration.
6 Cf. *Compendium of Social Doctrine,* no. 474: "[O]ne must avoid falling into the error of believing that only the spreading of the benefits connected with the new techniques of biotechnology can solve the urgent problems of poverty and underdevelopment that still afflict so many countries on the planet."

magisterial pronouncement until further, well-known criteria have been met.

GENERAL THOUGHTS OF A CATHOLIC

In mid-November 2003, the Pontifical Council for Justice and Peace held a conference in Rome on "Genetically Modified Organisms and the Social Doctrine of the Church," bringing together 67 "international experts."[7] What I find really striking about the trend of the debate over GMOs among ethicists and scientists, exemplified in the reports I read about the conference, is the *economist premises* of most parties to the discussion. The first questions are rarely disinterested ones such as: Are GMOs potentially disastrous for the environment and for the animals, including human beings, who will consume modified crops? Could such modifications be an assault on the integrity of created being? Is man authorized, even by his God-given dominion over nature, so to enter the innermost stuff of things and manipulate it? These are the questions that thinkers and believers pose. But the first questions in most discussions have tended to be: Can we find adequate ways of feeding the burgeoning poor of the Third World unless we have recourse to GMOs? Will GMOs help poorer countries lift themselves out of low productivity? In short, does the world economic situation *demand GMOs*? Thus, for example, Fr. Gonzalo Miranda, Dean of the School of

7 The proceedings of this conference have been published in a volume entitled *OGM: Minaccia o Speranza?* and published by ART. These proceedings join two earlier publications of importance for our subject: the Pontifical Academy for Life's *Animal and Plant Biotechnology: New Frontiers and New Responsibilities* (Libreria Editrice Vaticana, 1999) and the Pontifical Academy of Sciences' *Genetically Modified Plants for the Production of Food* (2001). Both of these may be regarded as generally in favor of genetic modification. The *Compendium of the Social Doctrine of the Church* (Libreria Editrice Vaticana, 2004) contains a section on biotechnologies, nn. 472–480. Finally, in September 2004, the Pontifical Academy of Sciences and the US Embassy to the Holy See sponsored another conference: "Feeding the Hungry: The Moral Imperative of Biotechnology." The build-up in pro-GM propaganda can be seen simply in the progression of the conference titles. One may be forgiven, I hope, for thinking Vatican officials guilty of naïveté; does it need to be pointed out to them that huge American commercial and political interests are at stake in the deployment of GMOs?

Bioethics of the Regina Apostolorum Pontifical Athenaeum, remarked in an interview: "If GMOs represent a real opportunity to foster the development of all countries, especially the neediest, it would be a real moral and solidaristic duty to favor their dissemination."[8] "Resistance is a mixed bag of hypersensitivity to food safety, and a European agenda of protectionism," commented US Ambassador to the Holy See, James Nicholson. "Meanwhile people are dying in Africa."[9]

Yet we cannot simply undertake, systematically and globally, what is unquestionably the most breathtaking human modification of the natural environment in the history of agriculture without thorough, long-term, international, multifaceted research into every aspect of the problem. Unfortunately, this is exactly what has not been done, and will not be done, as long as the wealthier regimes and their agri-business supporters are holding the reins. A revealing article by F. William Engdahl in *Current Concerns* summarizes the synergy that unites the interests of the most powerful nations and of the most aggressive GMO companies, such as Monsanto.[10] "Most shocking is the near total absence of fundamental independent research on the possible effects on humans and animals of introducing GM substances into the food chain," writes Engdahl, who goes on to summarize the few such studies that *have* been done, all of them warning urgently against the present rapid deployment of GMOs and identifying actual or potential GM-related damage to organisms. Engdahl also notes the unsettling, though not surprising, fact that unfavorable research has been quickly stifled by the combined pressure of commercial and political interests. Outspoken researchers have quickly lost their jobs.[11]

No wonder John Paul II, in a discourse on biological experimentation, warned against "every economic or political

8   https://zenit.org/2003/11/21/using-genetically-modified-organisms-could -be-a-duty-says-bioethicist/ Accessed July 26, 2020.
9   In an interview with Delia Gallagher for the Zenit News Service. It is to be noted that the US Embassy to the Holy See has played a front-ranking, even aggressive role in the promotion of GMOs at the Vatican.
10   See "Gene-manipulated Seeds: Are We Losing Our Food Security Too?" *Current Concerns*, July 2004, no. 4, p. 1.
11   *Ibid.*

opportunism which reproduces the schemes of an old colonialism in a new scientific and technical edition."[12] At the conference of November 2003, a similar warning was sounded by Fr. Roland Lesseps, formerly a professor at Loyola University in New Orleans and now a scientist in Zambia:

> There are other and more suitable ways to feed a hungry world than adopting a potentially dangerous technocratic approach. Food is not merely another economic commodity governed in its production and distribution by the laws of the market.... [G]enetic modification does not meet the tests of the social teaching of the Church for genuine integral development that respects human rights and the order of creation.

The spectre of consequentialism looms in pro-GMO arguments as in so many other arguments over global issues. No matter if we risk irreparable damage to the natural world; no matter if we risk unforeseen, gradual side-effects that our controlled experiments could not have revealed; no matter if we are gambling with the gift of creation — there are people who need food and so we've got to multiply it. The old-fashioned choices were bread from hard work and bread from heaven, one for the body, one for the soul. The new choice is bread from technology. It would be a dubious advance. The truth least often proclaimed in discussions of GMOs is the truth that matters most: the main guarantor of poverty in the Third World, the ultimate source of the profound social unrest, cultural flux, and government futility we see all over the globe, is not inadequate agricultural technology, much less overpopulation. It is social injustice rooted in massive political untruths. Due to First World colonialism and its modern version, the "global village" (which Timothy Radcliffe o.p has more aptly named the "global pillage"), starving people in one country are indirect slaves of wealthy people elsewhere, whose trash bins hold enough uneaten food to feed the poor twice over. One can often find the origins of misery and overcrowding, and one can always find their compounding agents, in the

12 *Insegnamenti* V. 3, 893 (see note 2 above).

theories of human life, of goods and values, state and society, money and commerce, espoused by Americans and Europeans of the modern age — theories that conveniently support the lifestyles of those who are "favored by fortune."

In company with all the modern popes, we must have the courage and clear-sightedness to address the *political-economic roots* of the Third World crisis. If we do not, how shall we resist the temptation whispered to us by the devil: "Use your money and brains to find a *technological* solution, and then you don't have to change your decadent way of life, you don't need to repudiate your ideologies! You can multiply bread in the wilderness. See, then, it's not a win-loss scenario, but a win-win; we don't have to fight over the pieces of a small pie, we just have to multiply the pies, and everybody will get some." It is a devil's bargain, for the devil is capable of guessing far better the effects of our selfish and short-sighted actions than we are, and he is only too glad to relieve temporary crises if he can gamble for long-term disasters. He will be pleased if multinational conglomerates can, by owning a greater and greater share of the world's *plant species,* dominate local economies and disenfranchise independent farmers.

At this point, someone might raise a double objection: first, that the entire world was "poor" a few centuries ago, not because of any exploitation but just because of a shortage of overall production; second, that capitalism, at its best, has increased the general sum of possessions across all classes, and at its worst, has merely enriched certain sectors and has left other sectors as they would always have been. This argument is fallacious. The miserable poverty that afflicts the masses in Mexico City or other such places in Latin America results from industrialization and urbanization, which are capitalist phenomena. The simple and honorable poverty in which most men have lived throughout most of history is not of the grinding, horrifying sort described by Dickens in *Hard Times.* On the other hand, it is true that not all poverty can be linked to Western structures of sin. Nevertheless, the links are more numerous and more profound than most people are aware of.

In any event, there can be much hypocrisy involved in this rhetoric about "we've got to help poor African countries produce more food, so let's genetically modify crops to produce bigger yields." The real problem is not whether you can get fifty bushels or one hundred bushels from a field of wheat. The real problem, as the social encyclicals point out, is structures of sin. One hundred bushels of wheat will fill some bellies over a short period; it won't dissolve the structures that led to mass poverty in the first place. Every Catholic has to bear witness that the crisis of the poor in the Third World and elsewhere is, to a large extent, our own fault—the fault of colonizers and neo-imperialists, of ideologies imported from Europe and America, of efforts to "help out" with contraceptives—and will never clear up until we reform ourselves.

Moreover, let us not lose sight of the less-than-honorable motivations of major GMO proponents, who are well positioned to profit enormously from the success of their enterprise. Is it not a flagrant violation of social justice that a company should *own* a species of plant and *charge* people for its ongoing use? In the past, a company has sold seeds to a farmer, and then the farmer owned the seeds and their produce. By contrast, a GM seed is patented, and the company that designed it holds a stake in all the future seed that bears this genetic signature. It seems, too, that techniques have been developed for designing seeds with an internal shut-down mechanism, so that after a number of generations the species would become infertile, compelling repurchase from the original manufacturer. With such tactics, it will not be long before the world's farmers gather in droves to pay their tithes to the Lords of Monsanto.

PARTICULAR THOUGHTS OF A PHILOSOPHER

At first glance, the theory of evolution might seem to support the view that modifying an organism isn't a big deal. After all, the evolutionist assumes that "Nature" has been modifying organisms more or less at random for millions of years, and the world is all right. Why can't man play the role of natural selection, and "select" in favor of a bigger soybean, a worm-proof corn? I will say a little later why human beings are foolish to try to "imitate Nature" in *this* manner, but it seems to me that this kind of evolutionary thinking remains at the surface of things, and does not engage the perennial issues.

If one takes seriously the Aristotelian-Thomistic notion of substantial form, to manipulate the material elements of a thing is an assault on its formal integrity. On Aristotelian grounds, no one can actually modify a substantial form. But a scientist can certainly change the material elements, the "stuff", because that is what our scientific instruments give us access to. No one can make me more or less a man, or change what it means to be a man, but he can chop off my arm, or reshape my nose, or pump drugs or hormones into me, or transplant an organ into my body. So too with plants: one can engineer their "stuff", their DNA, but this will not ever bring about more than a variety, or at most, a combination of two closely-related organisms, or a modification of one species by some trait belonging to another species.

It is never *the species* in the philosophical sense that is being changed, but rather the coding that regulates the material unfolding of what is precontained in the form. And forms, as St. Augustine and St. Thomas Aquinas recognized, can hold within themselves great capacities for development that are not always actualized. So there is plenty of room in the traditional philosophy of nature to account for the kind of experimentation geneticists are doing and the results they get, just as there is ample room in Thomistic metaphysics for the kind of developments that scientists typically claim as evidence for evolution.

The problem is, for every change we make, we risk initiating a snowball effect in future generations that we cannot expect to know ahead of time. How could we know, with certainty, what our changes will provoke — in other plants, in insects, in animals who eat the crops, in people who eat the crops or the animals? When modified corn and soybeans test-planted in northern Europe got mixed up with regular plants, and hence got into the food supply of the animals, people in those regions began to suffer hitherto unknown food allergies. This is not surprising. Allergies occur when the body rejects some organic matter deemed foreign, potentially dangerous; "this is something we can't deal with," the body's systems are saying. The whole natural world could be ready to cry out, similarly, "these artificially-modified organisms are not something we can deal with in the long run!"

Even if genetic manipulation of an organism is not in itself morally off limits, a basic reverence for creation as it comes from God's hands — respect for the natures that things have, awareness of the limits of organic tolerance, caution about unforeseen consequences — should be at work to dampen our enthusiasm for the project. A failure to cultivate an appropriately cautious attitude would itself be a sin against prudence, whatever may be said of the scientific procedures involved. Let's *not* try to make a plant bigger, stronger, more resistant, more winter-proof, etc. Instead let's use, with ingenuity and a spirit of gratitude, what is already available in the ecosystem. If some version of the evolutionary hypothesis is true, then the world has evolved what it can deal with right now. If that hypothesis is false, *a fortiori* the species we've got are what God intends for the world, at least at this time. In either case, technological interference is a bad idea and deserves opposition. Even if there were a slight *chance* of serious long-term problems, that would be more than sufficient to defeat the wisdom of GMO implementation.

One wishes that the Pontifical Council for Justice and Peace would get some heavy-duty moral theologians and natural philosophers down in Rome to *wrestle* with the big questions, unencumbered by prior political commitments.[13] Perhaps their reflection would lead them to advocate a stance of utmost vigilance, out of a legitimate love for the natural world, that fragile, magnificent gift of God. Respect for God's creation would seem to demand, at very least, that one should not tamper with the genetic structure of living things. That is their inner sanctuary. As Wendell Berry recounts:

> Wes Jackson of the Land Institute said once, thinking of the nuclear power and genetic engineering industries, "We ought to stay out of the nuclei." I remember that because I felt that he was voicing, not scientific intelligence, but a wise instinct: an intuition, common enough among human beings,

13   See notes 5 and 7 above.

that some things are and ought to be forbidden to us, off-limits, unthinkable, foreign, *properly* strange.

Berry goes on to note the naiveté of believing in, or the hypocrisy of appealing to, the "freedom" and "neutrality" of scientific research:

> A good many people, presumably, would have chosen to "stay out of the nuclei," but that was a choice they did not have. When a few scientists decided to go in, they decided for everybody. This "freedom of scientific inquiry" was immediately translated into the freedom of corporate and/or governmental exploitation. And so the freedom of the originators and exploiters has become, in effect, the abduction and imprisonment of all the rest of us. Adam was the first, but not the last, to choose for the whole human race.[14]

OBJECTIONS AND REPLIES

Let us return to the most common objection against my view. "Feeding the poor is so pressing a task, so noble an end, that it fully justifies the use of whatever means are available, unless there is something intrinsically immoral about them. Thus, if you cannot prove to me that GMOs are simply immoral, I conclude that their use is mandated."

The flaw in the argument is this. It may be the case that a particular GMO seed will not, as a matter of fact, prove environmentally harmful. However, unless we are certain of this fact, and in general, until we could be certain that we are genuinely *entitled*, as stewards of the natural world, to break into and modify the fundamental structures of things, we have an obligation to exercise extreme caution and to refrain from activity. The application of technology without adequate assurance of safety is itself immoral. What would constitute adequate assurance in a matter as subtle, complex, and grave as this one is probably such that it could never, in principle, be attained, and so the legitimacy of using GMO products would remain perpetually questionable.

14 *Life is a Miracle: An Essay Against Modern Superstition* (Washington: Counterpoint, 2001), pp. 76–77.

The burden of my argument is this: genetic modification ought to worry people simply because of *what it is*—a way of manipulating natural codes we do not fully understand, with effects we may not be able to envision much less control. All that we do is going to be irreversibly perpetuated in the wild once the seeds are out there, as has already happened and will continue to happen at an accelerating pace.[15] This is a much more serious matter than, say, pollution caused by cars or airplanes. All engines cause pollution, and pollution in general is a bad thing. But there is only a remote connection between the use of any particular machine and the harm of the earth's atmosphere. The atmosphere can handle a lot of pollution, pollution isn't self-reproducing, and finally, we and our animals don't directly consume pollution, though it affects us in a variety of ways. With GM seeds intended for the open fields—seeds that will grow into plants bearing many more seeds, until, by predictable patterns of consumption and random distribution, these new varieties come to be present in the entire food supply—there is a far more immediate, and a far deeper, concern.

To turn the objection on its head: if you cannot tell me that you are certain that this exercise of mastery over nature will *not* be a catastrophe in the long run, I can argue with considerable probability that it is immoral to attempt it. Something similar can be said about the development of nuclear weapons. Had the physicists in question known or even suspected what they were going to end up with, this foreknowledge would have rendered gravely immoral any effort of theirs directed toward inventing a nuclear weapon. Had they known or suspected the future evil, perhaps they would never have consented to begin the project, let alone bring it to completion. Perhaps. One wonders if modern man will ever learn his lessons.

A related objection would run like this: "Maybe I don't know enough about GMOs, but I don't see a clear line in your argument to separate the high-tech processes from the things that farmers routinely to do make their crops richer and sturdier. After all, if you design a disease-resistant carrot

---

15 See the summary of inevitable GM crop pollution in Engdahl, "Gene-manipulated Seeds," p. 1.

or something like that, aren't you *perfecting* a thing, and so bringing it closer to its ideal condition? At any rate, we have a divine mandate to subdue the earth, presumably meaning that we should harness nature's forces to serve the legitimate needs of mankind. I don't find a compelling argument that gene modification crosses a clear moral threshold."[16]

My response is this. What farmers have always done is to combine or separate strains already given in nature, to make a stronger plant with bigger yield, and so forth. This new strain, though produced by artful interventions, is no less natural, and no more a product of human engineering strictly speaking, than the original strains. Breeders do the same with animals to produce "better" varieties. Whatever the change may be — a healthier grain with a bigger yield, a new strain of rose with a captivating scent, a fatter and meatier pig — man has stayed out of the nucleus; he has not profaned the sanctuary where an organism's destiny is determined. He has merely, though cleverly, orchestrated *which* genes, among those that are naturally present, are going to dominate through reproduction. Breeding brings into proximity strains that could have naturally bred; whatever the results are, they are entirely *secundum naturam* — in accord, that is, with the natures of the organisms. Specialized crops or bred animals, when released into the wild to mingle with native varieties, revert to native characteristics with surprising swiftness. That is because nothing was really *done to* the genetic blueprint of the species; its possibilities were artfully drawn out, and nature can just as easily draw them back in.

Genetic modification, in contrast, is an "inside" operation that touches on the most fundamental material identity of an

16 The words in the Book of Genesis about *subduing* and *having dominion over the earth* (cf. 1:26–28) have got to be among the most badly abused verses in the entire sacred book. Listen, for example, to how Fr. Gonzalo Miranda glosses it: "Some people think that genetic manipulation of living beings is an ethically reprehensible act because it tends to alter what is natural, but the Church's anthropological view leads to different conclusions.... God has put man as a gardener of creation, who must act with responsibility to cultivate and take care of creation." Do we not encounter in these words the fallacy that Greek logicians long ago called *begging the question*?

organism, the "program" it follows in living. We have now the *power* to do this, but have we the *warrant*? Compare atomic energy and nuclear bombs: we discovered how to make a radioactive explosion equivalent to thousands of conventional bombs, but can we, by any stretch of reasoning, seriously maintain that this was part of our divine mandate to subdue the earth? It is, on the contrary, a perversion of our godlike image, a "playing at God" rather than a cooperation with him. If we were not habituated from childhood to place an implicit trust in all the goals and means of scientific research, we would feel an instinctive repugnance to the very idea of "modifying organisms." Berry quotes apposite lines from C. S. Lewis's *That Hideous Strength*: "Dreams of the far future destiny of man were dragging up from its shallow and unquiet grave the old dream of Man as God. The very experiences of the dissecting room and the pathological laboratory [one would have to add now: the geneticist's laboratory] were breeding a conviction that the stifling of all deep-set repugnancies was the first essential for progress."[17]

The goal of producing the "perfect carrot" is another example of Cartesian idealism, as if the natures of material things were indefinitely perfectible, as if man for his part could find the key to an endless perfectibility, appealing to "compassion for the poor" as his motivation (though in one's idealism, one shouldn't forget about owners and investors who would collect a handsome profit from sales of "perfect carrot" seed).

I am all in favor of measures for the poor, even radical ones; but the Church has never ceased to preach, and to demonstrate in action, that the measures must be above all social and spiritual, not technological. A technological solution is often a way of keeping bad lifestyles intact while stopping up the cracks in the dam so that the inevitable collapse of Western capitalist culture can be postponed a little while longer. Getting back to carrots: God created the carrot's nature, whether directly by a creative act, or mediately through *virtutes seminales* implanted in more basic creatures. In either case, it exists *as* he wishes it to exist in the ecosystem. Maybe

17   Cited in *Life is a Miracle*, p. 75.

the carrot's imperfections, if it has any that a carrot shouldn't have, are linked to the fall of man, since the whole of nature mysteriously fell when its lord and master fell; maybe they stem merely from the inevitable imperfection of each and every material thing as such, since prime matter is an indeterminate potency that substantial form cannot altogether master. In either case, the carrot (or any other species) in its very limitations is more than sufficient for our needs, if we farm according to sound agricultural principles. By trying to improve upon it *from within,* we cross the line from stewardship, which receives thankfully and works diligently, to an arrogant emulation of God's creative power.

In the final analysis, GMOs are a potent manifestation of the attitude of the "mastery of nature" found in Francis Bacon and René Descartes, which is plainly Luciferian and in no way Christian. For Bacon, final causality exists only in the case of man, who freely acts for an end. In the case of other bodies, finality must be totally dismissed, for it is no more than a misleading metaphor. Bacon thus denies that anything in the natural world truly acts for an end. But if nature has no end, if it is simply malleable matter, there could be nothing wrong with reshaping it to correspond, as closely as technology allows, to *man's* freely-chosen intentions. One might even say that if something doesn't have an end, it is a good thing to *give* it one. The male chauvinists used to say: "A woman needs a man to give her direction." Similarly, the Baconian master of nature says: "What we call 'plants' and 'animals' are just raw materials waiting to be directed, channeled, *used.*" The moment we let go of formal and final causalities, the basis for ethical limitations is abandoned. If a plant or animal has no nature or essence — if it is simply matter obeying laws — then there is no reason why man, who has discovered those laws, should not reconstitute the matter as he wishes, for his own purposes. There is simply nothing else that deserves to be taken into consideration.

To be skeptical about this attitude does not mean that one must be a romantic or a purist toward the natural world, viewing human intervention as necessarily or even generally bad, and, in contrast, thinking it optimal to leave everything untouched in its wild state. Were this true, even primitive agriculture would count as a betrayal of naturalness, and hunting and gathering would count as aggression. But there is good reason to see the *modern* (post-Reformation) attitude toward and treatment of nature as a departure from a healthy Catholic attitude, which recognizes in the world *both* a metaphysical symbol of the beauty of God and a storehouse for human needs, an incentive to human industry. This is what one finds, for example, in St. Bonaventure's authentically Franciscan cosmology.[18]

When we are uncertain about what is right and what is wrong on a difficult issue, we must not abdicate our social responsibility out of awe before the high priests of statecraft or salesmanship, but keep our freedom of judgment intact while searching for the truth. At all costs we should not fall prey to the universal assumption that we might as well try out new technology even if we still have some disturbing questions about its long-term consequences; "we *can* do it, therefore we *should* do it." This is what got us nuclear weapons, contraceptives, and other technological burdens. It might prove no different with GMOs. As Fr. Lawrence Dewan o.p. has written: "some technical devices, viewed not merely as works of art but as expressions of total human appetite, can be the very embodiment of perversion. Technology can be put in the service of virtue, but it can also be put in the service of vice, i.e. greed, unscrupulous power, the lascivious life, massive injustice."[19]

My plea, then, is a plea for caution, for serious investigation, for clear thinking. Without this, we may stumble ahead, with all our good intentions, into a major ecological crisis for which absolutely no remedy exists.

18   See my article "The World as Symbol of Divine Beauty in the Thought of St. Bonaventure," *Faith & Reason* 24/25 (1999–2000), pp. 31–54.
19   "Antimodern, Ultramodern, Postmodern: A Plea for the Perennial," *Etudes Maritainiennes \ Maritain Studies* 9 (1993), pp. 7–28; 24. Fr. Dewan goes on to say: "Technology, by virtue of the very richness it has attained to in our time, forces us to face up to the essence of morality, to ask what questions we should really be asking. Should we merely consider: is the undertaking feasible? Will it work? Or will we be the sort of people who ask whether it is a procedure which accords with a noble idea of humanity?"

9

Laudato Si' *and the Critique of the Technocratic Paradigm*

THOMAS STORCK

POPE FRANCIS' ENCYCLICAL *LAUDATO si'* of May 2015 is the first major document of the magisterium devoted to our material environment, "on care for our common home," as the formal title of the encyclical runs. But this hardly means that the document or its contents constitutes an innovation in Catholic thought. Speaking only of magisterial documents, we find numerous pronouncements of St. John Paul II and Benedict XVI devoted to the subject, including large sections of Benedict's 2009 encyclical *Caritas in Veritate*, as well as several sections of the *Catechism of the Catholic Church* that set forth the fundamental principles for a Catholic view of the natural environment. But well before the Church had officially taken notice of the damage that mankind was afflicting on its God-given home, individual Catholic writers of note had already called attention to environmental degradation. Christopher Dawson, for example, wrote as long ago as 1935 of "the very face of nature [being] changed by the destruction of the countryside and the pollution of the earth and the air and the waters."[1] And the Irish priest, Fr. Denis Fahey, in his 1953 book, *The Church and Farming*, devoted considerable space to what he called "the ravages of agri-industry," and included an entire chapter which discussed in considerable detail the benefits of organic farming and the deleterious effects of chemical fertilizers.[2] Indeed, Fr. Fahey explained the Cartesian roots of modern

---

1 "Catholicism and the Bourgeois Mind" in John J. Mulloy, ed., *Dynamics of World History*, (La Salle, Ill.: Sherwood Sugden, 1978), p. 203.
2 Denis Fahey, *The Church and Farming* (Hawthorne, CA: Omni/Christian Book Club, [1953] 1988), p. 89, and see chap. III, pp. 98–114.

farming, and contrasted the philosophy underlying these destructive practices with principles drawn from the philosophy of St. Thomas Aquinas.

It is hardly surprising that it took some time for the Church herself, on an official level, to turn her attention to these problems, since they were not widely recognized until the 1960s. Pope Francis, however, has done a service to the Church and put together in one document so many of the principles, drawn from both reason and revelation, that should guide us in thinking about the environment, and as such serve as the ethical basis for our behavior toward the created world around us.

There is much of interest in *Laudato si'*, including a restatement of the fundamental principle of Catholic social teaching as enunciated by popes from Leo XIII to Benedict XVI and Francis, that economic efficiency, as that is understood by most economists, still less the interests and profits of the powerful, cannot rightly override the economy's primary function of serving the well-being of mankind as a whole. For the most part, however, Pope Francis discusses Catholic social doctrine here as that pertains to our impact on the environment, and so I intend to focus on what seems to me the encyclical's major achievement, its penetrating critique of what he calls the *technocratic paradigm*, the fundamental way that our civilization, including its economic system, thinks about and makes use of technology in its attempt to dominate the natural world. This discussion is centered in sections 106 through 114 of the encyclical.

Section 106 presents the basic points of this critique as follows:

> [H]umanity has taken up technology and its development *according to an undifferentiated and one-dimensional paradigm*. This paradigm exalts the concept of a subject who, using logical and rational procedures, progressively approaches and gains control over an external object. This subject makes every effort to establish the scientific and experimental method, which in itself is already a technique of possession, mastery, and transformation.... Men

and women have constantly intervened in nature, but for a long time this meant being in tune with and respecting the possibilities offered by the things themselves. It was a matter of receiving what nature itself allowed, as if from its own hand. Now, by contrast, we are the ones to lay our hands on things, attempting to extract everything possible from them while frequently ignoring or forgetting the reality in front of us. Human beings and material objects no longer extend a friendly hand to one another; the relationship has become confrontational. This has made it easy to accept the idea of infinite or unlimited growth, which proves so attractive to economists, financiers, and experts in technology.

Modern man is almost drunken with his ability to dominate and control nature with the "technique of possession, mastery, and transformation." According to this understanding of man's relationship with his environment, the latter exists solely in order to be used by us, but not simply by "receiving what nature itself allowed, as if from its own hand," but by exploiting and "attempting to extract everything possible from [nature] while frequently ignoring or forgetting the reality in front of us." It is not a matter of working *with* nature, but of twisting her and wresting from her not only what is in accord with her natural potentialities, but of anything and everything which our technique can manage to extort.

This has affected even the way we think. Section 107 notes the "tendency... to make the method and aims of science and technology an epistemological paradigm...." It not only becomes very difficult for many people to imagine ways of dealing with the dilemmas of human existence which do not involve exploitative technology, but even worse, too many think that it is by technology alone that such difficulties can be dealt with. "Our capacity to make decisions, a more genuine freedom, and the space for each one's alternative creativity are diminished" (108).

Both those who look favorably on the consumption of genetically modified food and those who support the use of drugs or surgery to alter a person's sexual characteristics according to the supposed demands of his "gender identity," are equally slaves of this technocratic way of thinking. To both groups there is nothing strange about human actions which directly mutilate or distort what nature presents to us. In the former case we show how little we respect the varying natures of created things, their natural capacities and inclinations, the possible dangers inherent in interfering with them,[3] and in the latter we subordinate the created bodily structure of the human person to an act of human hubris and will, showing not the slightest interest in finding out why anyone might feel so alienated from his own body as to wish to violently alter it chemically or surgically, nor what such alienation might indicate about his psychic health.[4] It is impossible or very difficult for those enslaved to the technocratic paradigm to think that there is any other way of providing for man's needs other than by "a technique of possession, mastery, and transformation."

Francis also points out the cumulative effect of our technological decisions on our ways of living.

> We have to accept that technological products are not neutral, for they create a framework which ends up conditioning lifestyles and shaping social possibilities along the lines dictated by the interests of certain powerful groups. Decisions which may seem purely instrumental are in reality decisions about the kind of society we want to build. (107)

We have built our entire society upon these technological premises, especially in North America. Multi-lane highways and ever more numerous parking lots are only two of the more obvious ways in which we have altered the physical environment itself in accord with the perceived imperatives of our technology, in blind and unthinking obedience to its

3   See sections 133–34 of the encyclical for a specific treatment of genetically modified food.
4   For an interesting but disturbing discussion of the mind's ability to be at odds with the integrity and meaning of the body, see Carl Elliott, "A New Way to be Mad," *The Atlantic*, December 2000. Online at https://www.theatlantic.com/magazine/archive/2000/12/a-new-way-to-be-mad/304671/ Accessed August 1, 2020.

demands. Instead of asking whether it is a healthy and wise use of land — a gift from the Creator which is irreplaceable and strictly limited — to pave over farmland or woods or meadows for an ever-growing number of automobiles, we take the path of least resistance, and refuse to consider the possibility of making any far-reaching changes in our way of living. Thus with every decision we become more dependent on the structures and limits created by our previous decisions, so dependent that we cannot imagine any other way of living and organizing society. We forget that every technological decision tends to create a way of life, or strengthens one already in existence, which then becomes all the more difficult to undo or reverse later on. "The effects of this model on reality as a whole, human and social, are seen in the deterioration of the environment, but this is just one sign of a reductionism which affects every aspect of human and social life." Of course, none of this is to say that technological development *as such* is evil, but rather that technology, like all products of fallen humanity, must be judged on more than its ability to do something faster, cheaper or easier, but rather according to its impact on human life, individually and corporately, and on the natural environment as well, and that an attitude of mind which sees the created world as simply raw material for man's exploitation is wrong.

In section 110 Francis takes up one of the ways of thinking which is in part a direct result of this technological paradigm.

> The specialization which belongs to technology makes it difficult to see the larger picture. The fragmentation of knowledge proves helpful for concrete applications, yet it often leads to a loss of appreciation for the whole, for the relationships between things, and for the broader horizon, which then becomes irrelevant.

Technology and the kind of science upon which it is built are very adept at breaking down a perceived difficulty into its constituent parts, and at devising methods of overcoming these difficulties. But as to whether or why the difficulty should be overcome, such science knows nothing and can know nothing. It simply assumes a technocratic solution to the difficulty. Thus any difficulty becomes simply a "problem" to be solved by the invention or application of technology, in the cheapest and fastest way possible. Any effects such use of technology has on mankind, on our culture and the world around us or even our physical health, is of little or no interest.

In response to this oppressive technocratic reasoning Francis proposes nothing less than "a distinctive way of looking at things, a way of thinking, policies, an educational program, a lifestyle and a spirituality which together generate resistance to the assault of the technocratic paradigm." What such a "resistance" might mean, the Pontiff suggests later in the encyclical beginning in section 191, where he writes, "But we need to grow in the conviction that a decrease in the pace of production and consumption can at times give rise to another form of progress and development." For many people any suggestion that "a decrease in the pace of production and consumption" could ever be a rational choice seems simply madness, but that is because such people have already surrendered to the logic both of technology and of the market. While it is true that many in the world exist in poverty, it is not primarily they who are consumed with the desire for ever more and more goods. The ordinary materialist American way of looking at this is well expressed in the following by the well-known economist, the late Paul Samuelson.

> An objective observer would have to agree that, even after two centuries of rapid economic growth, production in the United States is simply not high enough to meet everyone's desires. If you add up all the wants, you quickly find that there are simply not enough goods and services to satisfy even a small fraction of everyone's consumption desires. Our national output would have to be many times larger before the average American could live at the level of the average doctor or big-league baseball player.[5]

5 Paul Samuelson, *Microeconomics* (Boston: McGraw-Hill, 17th ed., 2001), p. 4.

It is simply assumed here that the claimed desire of everyone to "live at the level of the average doctor or big-league baseball player" must be accepted without demur. This in itself is a good example of how a social or human science such as economics, modeling itself on the technique of technocratic physical science, simply assumes its aims as given and considers its task merely as generating means to satisfy those aims. Economics, as understood by the majority of its practitioners today, looks upon the world with a kind of tunnel vision, never asking what the point is of piling up stuff and more stuff, other than the fulfilling of man's limitless desires. (This is to omit mention of its blindness toward the fact that those who possess economic and political power will almost always shape an economy in the direction of fulfilling *their* limitless desires, at the expense of the rest of us.)

In section 114 Francis repeats with a slightly different emphasis what he said earlier, "Science and technology are not neutral; from the beginning to the end of a process, various intentions are in play and can take on distinct shapes." The intentions of those who hold power almost always affect not only the use of technology, but the very inventions themselves. It is not an accident, for example, that expensive research, much of it funded by government, has gone into creating farm machinery unsuited for small farms, but designed to increase the profits of agri-business.[6] This fact might remind us of one of the major themes of C. S. Lewis' novel, *That Hideous Strength.* There Professor Filostrato avows to Mark Studdock, "All that talk about the power of Man over Nature — Man

6   "It is the largest-scale growers, the farm machinery and chemicals input companies and the processors who are the primary beneficiaries. Machinery companies . . . almost continually engage in cooperative research efforts at land grant colleges. These corporations contribute money and some of their own research personnel to help land grant scientists develop machinery. . . . In some cases they actually receive exclusive licenses to manufacture and sell the products of tax-paid research. . . . "Independent family farmers also have been largely ignored by the land grant colleges. Mechanization research by land grant colleges is either irrelevant or only incidentally adaptable to the needs of 87 to 99 percent of America's farmers." Agribusiness Accountability Project, quoted in Wendell Berry, *The Unsettling of America: Culture & Agriculture* (New York: Avon, c. 1977), pp. 149–50.

in the abstract—is only for the *canaglia*. You know as well as I do that Man's power over Nature means the power of some men over other men with Nature as the instrument."7 And as Lewis points out as well in his book, *The Abolition of Man*, the kind of science that has created the technocratic paradigm is not content to work upon the external world. Man himself is its next and perhaps last object. For as Henri de Lubac put it, "But, since man, too, had become an object of science like all the rest, why would what was true for the external world be any less true for man himself?"8

If we look more specifically at some of the suggested ways of resisting the technological imperative which Francis offers beginning in section 191, these may be summed up in calling for the

> need to change "models of global development"; this will entail a responsible reflection on "the meaning of the economy and its goals with an eye to correcting its malfunctions and misapplications". It is not enough to balance, in the medium term, the protection of nature with financial gain, or the preservation of the environment with progress. Halfway measures simply delay the inevitable disaster. Put simply, it is a matter of redefining our notion of progress. A technological and economic development which does not leave in its wake a better world and an integrally higher quality of life cannot be considered progress. Frequently, in fact, people's quality of life actually diminishes—by the deterioration of the environment, the low quality of food or the depletion of resources—in the midst of economic growth. In this context, talk of sustainable growth usually becomes a way of distracting attention and offering excuses. It absorbs the language and values of ecology into the categories of finance and technocracy, and the social and environmental responsibility of businesses

---

7 *That Hideous Strength* (New York: Macmillan, 1965), p. 178.
8 Henri de Lubac, *The Drama of Atheist Humanism*, (San Francisco: Ignatius, [1949] 1995), p. 406.

often gets reduced to a series of marketing and image-enhancing measures. (194)

The principle of the maximization of profits, frequently isolated from other considerations, reflects a misunderstanding of the very concept of the economy. As long as production is increased, little concern is given to whether it is at the cost of future resources or the health of the environment; as long as the clearing of a forest increases production, no one calculates the losses entailed in the desertification of the land, the harm done to biodiversity or the increased pollution. In a word, businesses profit by calculating and paying only a fraction of the costs involved. Yet only when "the economic and social costs of using up shared environmental resources are recognized with transparency and fully borne by those who incur them, not by other peoples or future generations", can those actions be considered ethical. (195)

In other words, the first task, always a difficult task, is to reorient out thinking, for unless we think correctly we will not act correctly. No one can pretend that such a reorientation can be accomplished without effort, not the least because it would involve disturbing the interests of many powerful persons who will do their utmost to resist any such changes. But it is nonetheless an imperative, not only for the safeguarding of the natural world, but of ourselves as well. For once the human mind is shaped by the technocratic paradigm it looks upon everything it surveys as simply material for manipulation. There is no logical reason to say about any portion of the created world, "Hands off!" What is required in order to resist and reverse this way of thinking is first to realize that it is poisoned at its root. If we think of any part of nature as merely material from which "to extract everything possible," then we will soon think that way about everything, including ourselves. Let us seek then, however impossible it might seem, to "generate resistance to the assault of the technocratic paradigm," to propose another way of thinking and living to our fellow men, a way that for Catholics at least ought to be the connatural and obvious way of living, consistent with the deepest insights of our philosophical and theological tradition. That there are environmentalists whose principles are anything but those of sound philosophy need not disturb us, for we can champion this resistance based on our own traditions, on the thinking of St. Thomas, on the settled teachings of moral theology, and perhaps we can even teach others that there are better principles than those they know by which to promote "care for our common home." In any case, both present exigencies and the moral demands of the Faith leave us little choice: We must resist the technocratic paradigm or become victims of it ourselves.

Listening with an
Attentive Ear to God's Poetry

PETER A. KWASNIEWSKI

O NE MORNING, IN THE MIDDLE OF A
winter in Austria, I leaned out of my office window
and looked out upon the surrounding mountains,
the silent trees, the snow hidden in clefts of rock, the solitary
raven perched on a high branch. As my ears grew attuned to
the quiet of the world, I heard the chirping of unseen birds
and the faint sound of the wind blowing across the field. I
saw four sparrows flying in perfect formation, a leaf skimming
along the ground. The sky was grey. Things were somehow
still and in motion, restless and at peace. It was for me a
moment of wonder: so beautiful, so inexhaustible are these
things—every single one of them speaking of God.

This, I imagine, is the sort of experience that prompted
Gerard Manley Hopkins, SJ, to write one of his most famous
poems, "God's Grandeur,"

> The world is charged with the grandeur of God.
>   It will flame out, like shining from shook foil;
>   It gathers to a greatness, like the ooze of oil
> Crushed. Why do men then now not reck his rod?
> Generations have trod, have trod, have trod;
>   And all is seared with trade; bleared, smeared
>   with toil;
>   And wears man's smudge and shares man's smell:
>   the soil
> Is bare now, nor can foot feel, being shod.
>
> And for all this, nature is never spent;
>   There lives the dearest freshness deep down
>   things;

And though the last lights off the black West went
　Oh, morning, at the brown brink eastward,
　　springs—
Because the Holy Ghost over the bent
　World broods with warm breast and with ah!
　bright wings.

It is no secret that theology has suffered a tremendous
decline in modern times. Yes, there are very fine individual
teachers and authors, but as a discipline it has lost its queenly
place among the sciences, its grandeur, its profundity, when
we compare it with the great Fathers and Doctors of the
Church. The same may be said of Catholic spirituality: were
we to place most of the popular spiritual books published
today in a balance, with the classics of mysticism in the other
tray, no one can truly be surprised at how the balance will
tilt. (In the following, I will speak of "theology" but I intend
it to include spirituality as well.)

Can we explain this decrepitude? Generalizations are risky,
but I nevertheless believe it to be true that theology is moribund because metaphysics or the study of being is moribund;
metaphysics is moribund, because the philosophy of nature
is moribund; the philosophy of nature is moribund because
natural history, that is, carefully paying attention to natural
things in their natural environments, is moribund; and this
is so, because men are no longer *looking* and *listening* to the
world, but watching television, reading newspapers, bending
like slaves over the work desk or popping instant dinners into
the microwave.

The only way that richly Catholic, profoundly speculative,
affective theology will once again blossom is by a renewed
immersion in the good and beautiful creation of God.

This is what Saint Augustine did: think of the famous
passage in the *Confessions* where he poses his deepest questions to the world around him, and that world gives him
an answer, because he is truly *listening* to it. This is what
Saint Thomas Aquinas did, too. St. Teresa Benedicta of the
Cross (the religious name of Edith Stein) says that God is the

primary theologian and the world is his theological *Summa*. In like manner Ronald McArthur, one of the founders of Thomas Aquinas College, claimed that Augustinian interiority is fundamentally different from Cartesian interiority because Augustine looks upon himself, as upon the world, with the warm wonder of a lover seeking his lost beloved, not with the cold gaze of rationalism that freezes whatever it looks at. Augustine, in other words, is looking for truth and understanding, Descartes for mastery and power.

Especially nowadays, people, in addition to living cut off from a "naked" experience of reality, can also make themselves blind to that which is to be seen or heard when they adhere to preconceived theories that render the mind incapable of making sense out of what the outer and inner senses present to it by way of experience. Put differently, it is possible for pseudo-science and ideology to paralyze or impede the intellect's progression to the natural judgments on which the upward progress to theology relies.

That such a blindness can happen was obvious even to the pagan Greeks. In Book IV of his *Metaphysics,* Aristotle refutes the relativist who says—and maybe even convinces himself that he really *thinks*—that something can both be and not be at the same time and in the same respect, thus undermining the possibility of any meaningful discourse, dialogue, and learning. Descartes might be taken as a vibrant example of this mental obtuseness (unless, of course, he was merely playing with his readers as a cat plays with a mouse) when he says in his *Meditations* that the people walking around the street outside the window might actually be automatons dressed up as men . . . for how could one really know otherwise?

This is the kind of swamp of confusion into which the undisciplined—or, as with the founder of analytic geometry, hypertrophically over-disciplined—intellect can sink. The typical modern man on the street has an undisciplined mind: he has been so brainwashed by errors, by swallowing contradictions of first principles, that he is not capable, in any habitual way, of making intellectual progress by a series of disciplined judgments and inferences.

A Descartes (or, to choose a more recent example, a Stephen Hawking) has, on the other hand, an unnaturally "disciplined" mind: so exclusively and narrowly is he trained in a certain way of thinking or a certain body of data, that he can no longer evaluate the full range of reality as it is given in spontaneous consciousness and apprehended by many different kinds of soul-acts. This is something Aristotle points out in *Metaphysics,* Book II, chapter 3. Once again, Aristotle is far ahead of us moderns, and that is one reason, among many, why liberal arts students should study Aristotle consistently and well.

Josef Pieper reminds us that creatures bear within themselves a trace of the incomprehensible mystery, the unfathomable depths, of their Creator. Gerard Manley Hopkins knew this and expressed it in brilliant verse. William Wordsworth knew it, too:

> It is a beauteous evening, calm and free,
> The holy time is quiet as a Nun
> Breathless with adoration; the broad sun
> Is sinking down in its tranquility;
> The gentleness of heaven broods o'er the Sea;
> Listen! the mighty Being is awake,
> And doth with his eternal motion make
> A sound like thunder—everlastingly.
>
> Dear child! dear Girl! that walkest with me here,
> If thou appear untouched by solemn thought,
> Thy nature is not therefore less divine:
> Thou liest in Abraham's bosom all the year;
> And worshipp'st at the Temple's inner shrine,
> God being with thee when we know it not.

Poets desire to have knowledge of *singulars* as such, of the very individuality of things in their real existence. They express this knowledge in descriptions and metaphors which, while being in tension with the goal of singling out unrepeatable experiences, nevertheless bring home to us the message and meaning of the world as a sequence of intelligible words that God is speaking to *me,* to *you,* at this very moment.

* * *

Looking over the landscape of late modernity, one can see a number of dominant trends of thought. Two of them, I believe, are especially pernicious: the attitude, brought about by a combination of materialism and technology, that sees all of nature—including human nature—as raw material for exploitation ("If we *can* do it, we *should* do it," or more classically expressed, "might makes right"); and the rise of a thousand vague "spiritualities" by which this selfish attitude is glossily packaged in a socially acceptable and psychologically self-deceptive manner. In other words, a do-it-yourself spirituality that is, at its core, still some form of egoistic hedonism.

How did we sink to this point, and how do we escape from it? There are many ways to answer those questions, but here I would like to approach it by contrasting three of Western history's most influential thinkers.

Sometimes called "the father of modern philosophy," René Descartes (1596–1650) in his mature writings repudiated the Catholic philosophy and theology he had learned at the Jesuit school of La Flèche. In this regard he exemplified one of the most notable traits of modern philosophers: their continual effort to find the perfect foundation on which to build their system, which requires departing from or even destroying the foundations already laid by others. It is the opposite of the Christian principle: "what I received I passed on to you as of first importance" (1 Cor. 15:3).

We can see this parting of ways in a famous passage from Descartes's *Discourse on Method*: "In place of that speculative philosophy taught in the schools, it is possible to find a practical philosophy," by means of which we could "render ourselves as *masters and possessors* of nature." Not, in other words, respectful students, custodians, and assistants of nature, who learn to work with it for our good and for the good of the whole, but rapists who overpower nature for their own pleasure, slave-drivers who subject creatures to their own wills. Why should we shift our attitude in this way? In the same work, Descartes tells us:

This is desirable not only for the invention of an infinity of devices that would enable one to enjoy trouble-free the fruits of the earth and all the goods found therein, but also principally for the maintenance of health, which unquestionably is the first good and the foundation of all the other goods of this life...[I]f it is possible to find some means to render men generally more wise and more adroit than they have been up until now, I believe that one should look for it in medicine.... [O]ne could rid oneself of an infinity of maladies, as much of the body as of the mind, and even perhaps also the frailty of old age, if one had a sufficient knowledge of their causes and of all the remedies that nature has provided us.

"An infinity of devices" for "enjoying trouble-free the fruits of the earth"? Here we have the blueprint of the technological and materialist revolution that implicitly or explicitly takes bodily health as the highest good or *summum bonum*, bodily suffering as the primary evil, and medicine as the supreme discipline. God is not so much fiercely rejected as he is ignored, or rather, shown the door because he does not deliver the immediate physical goods on which we set our hopes. This is what John Paul II would call "practical atheism."

In another work, *Principles of Philosophy*, Descartes compared philosophy to a tree whose root is metaphysics, whose trunk is physics, and whose three branches are medicine, mechanics, and morals. After introducing the metaphor, he writes: "Now just as it is not the roots or the trunk of a tree from which one gathers the fruit, but only the ends of the branches, so the principal benefit of philosophy depends on those parts of it which can only be learnt last of all." The fruit of knowledge is, on the bodily side, an abundance of devices for postponing or tranquilizing death and, on the psychic side, the gritty Stoicism to accept life in a universe of indifferent and impersonal forces.

One of the first to see that Cartesianism had nothing but this to offer mankind was Gottfried Wilhelm Leibniz (1646–1716), one of the inventors of calculus, who around

1679 wrote a perspicacious letter on God and the soul in the course of which he says:

> Descartes's God, or perfect being, is not a God like the one we imagine or hope for, that is, a God just and wise, doing everything possible for the good of creatures. Rather, Descartes's God is something approaching the God of Spinoza [which is identical with the impersonal cosmos] . . . That is why a God like Descartes's allows us no consolation other than that of patience through strength. . . . It is impossible to believe that this God cares for intelligent creatures any more than he does for the others; each creature will be happy or unhappy depending on how it finds itself engulfed in these great currents or vortices. Descartes has good reason to recommend, instead of felicity, patience without hope.

After centuries of optimistic Cartesian rationalism had run their course and the world seemed to have been emptied of meaning by materialism and stripped of mystery by technology, the philosopher Martin Heidegger (1889–1976) attempted to make a new beginning. Yet his response, presented as the polar opposite, shares in the same sickness: philosophy is being-towards-death, acknowledging and embracing the inevitability of annihilation. Genuine "care" for others and "authenticity" within oneself are established in this courageous welcoming of non-being. Is there not a strange resemblance between such thoughts and the program of enervation espoused by the "compassionate Buddha," the great teacher of spiritual euthanasia? Did the Christian West have to wait so long for a philosopher to give them the same message as the ancient Far East? And yet, without the virtues of the Far East, we are much more likely to take this message of despair as an excuse for a desperate clutching at evanescent pleasures: "Eat, drink, and be merry, for tomorrow you will die."

The wise folly or foolish wisdom of the Apostle Paul and of his medieval disciple Thomas Aquinas is as far removed from Cartesian pride or Heideggerian despair as the extremes of vice from the mean of virtue. Just as the lofty mountain rises far above the lowlands, the "mystical theism" of Aquinas, founded on the personal and transformative mystery of God, rises far above the practical atheism of Descartes and the speculative atheism of Heidegger. St. Thomas already saw their positions and rejected them, as he had done with thousands of other objections to the truth of the Christian religion and its metaphysical foundations.

No wonder Leo XIII, in his landmark encyclical *Aeterni Patris* of 1879, proposed him as the thinker most suited not only for replenishing the rickety curricula of seminaries and schools, but also for guiding the Church's creative philosophical and theological response to *modernity*. Pope Leo was advocating a creative fidelity to tradition — the exact opposite of the mentality of building from scratch that we saw in the father of modern philosophy.

* * *

"And he said to them: Go ye into the whole world, and preach the gospel to every creature" (Mark 16, 15). How do we preach the gospel to *every* creature — including stones, trees, brute animals?

We cause them to participate in the Gospel by elevating, as much as possible, each rank of being, through our cognition of them and our appreciation of their beauty, their intricacy, their strength, their usefulness; through domestication of them if they are susceptible to human reason in this manner; and through the sacred liturgy, when it takes up each order of being and harnesses it for the worship of God: a church built of stone, vessels made of metal, vestments woven of silk and linen, windows crafted from glass, flowers on the altar, the blessing of fields, livestock, gardens, and wine. We preach the Gospel to them by preaching it *through* them, thus making them partakers of the mission of the Word and of the Church.

The famous hymn of the *Benedicite*, taken from chapter 3 of the book of Daniel and incorporated into the Latin Divine Office, strongly underlines this truth. Whenever I pray it slowly enough and think about what I'm doing — addressing imperatives to all of creation! — something in the verses stirs a faint memory, fosters a present gratitude, and incites a longing for a new heavens and a new earth where righteousness will be at home.

More recently, I came across this exquisite passage in a book on Mother Catherine-Mectilde de Bar, foundress of the Benedictines of Perpetual Adoration:

> Man finds himself to be as the *heart* of creation. In our body, the heart is, in effect, only a small organ, and nevertheless it vivifies all the whole. In the same way, man, although tiny in the place he occupies on the earth, animates it in its totality. When the heart loves, it is the whole man that loves. And in the same way, when man adores his God, it is the whole universe that, in him, adores and glorifies its Creator. . . . Man is the priest of the universe: through his nature, at once bodily and spiritual, he is the intermediary between the visible world and the invisible world, between ponderous matter and the God who is Spirit. He alone is capable of offering that "worship in spirit and in truth" which the Father seeks and which Christ demands of the Samaritan woman for quenching the thirst of His Heart.

"Man is the priest of the universe . . . the intermediary between the visible and the invisible . . . " It is in just this spirit that St. Gertrude the Great prays:

> May my heart and my soul, with all the substance of my flesh, all my senses, and all the powers of my body and my mind, with all creatures, praise Thee and give Thee thanks, O sweet Lord, faithful lover of mankind, for thy infinite mercy!

Our Lord Jesus Christ, whose coming in the flesh and whose Second Coming in glory we recall each Advent season, is the Last Adam, the perfect Man, the divine Man, the Eternal High Priest — the one Mediator between God and man, visible and invisible, who could utter St. Gertrude's sentiments in a uniquely complete and exhaustive way. In the Son, "ponderous matter and the God who is Spirit" are united indivisibly, inseparably, unconfusedly. In the Heart of Jesus is the perfect glorification of God by material creation. His human knowledge of worldly things elevates them as no other man's knowledge can do. His love and use of them bestows upon them a dignity they could never have by themselves. In Christ the world encounters its Maker, returns to its origin, attains its end.

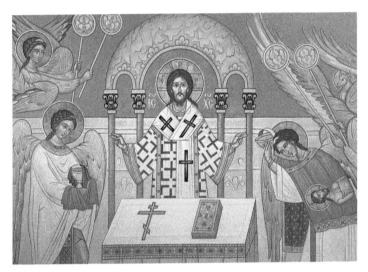

When Our Lord prayed the *Benedicite*, as he surely must have done, he was uttering to every thing and every kind of thing the echo of the creative word that called forth their realization *ex nihilo*, the vivifying word that sustains them in being, the commanding word that harnesses them for salvation, the fearsome word that dooms them to finitude and fire at the end of time. In the *Benedicite* uttered by his holy lips, the creature heard itself called as if by name, called to bend before the Name above all other names. In particular, the things taken up by Christ as the matter of the sacraments acquired special status: they became, as it were, the aristocracy of material beings, a rank they will occupy until the world is no more. They have become quasi-natural signs of their Mediator.

* * *

Although Catholics will always be drawn to Platonism, which has sometimes proved helpful (Augustine, Dionysius,

Maximus) and at other times perilous (Origen, Eriugena), there is a basic sense in which they will always be Aristotelians. On the one hand, Aristotle is an unbending realist: whatever I can see, hear, touch, taste, smell, feel, or otherwise perceive, is *real*; compared to these, concepts, memories, and imaginings are less real. On the other hand, Aristotle is an uncompromising spiritualist: God, the unseen, untouched, inaccessible, imperceptible object of pure thought is *the* Real, and the entire universe of bodies undergoing alteration, substantial change, and local motion is less real, emanating from him who is the First Principle, striving upwards towards him who is the Last End. Form and matter, the two great principles of all composites, are themselves unseen and untouched. We surmise their necessary presence, hidden though they are behind the veil of common experience.

The *here* and the *now* is our daily bread, our human sacrament. What is everywhere and always is difficult to penetrate, hard to recognize, noble beyond all words, wise beyond all thoughts, consoling to the immortal man. The concrete physical presence of the beloved is the focus, the goal, the fulfillment of the here and now, but it is only the beginning of the Real Presence, the spiritual omnipresence of the beloved, by which the here and the now is elevated, enlarged, suffused with intimations of eternity and ubiquity that not even (what mortals call) absence can forestall or weaken.

Touch is the only sense that puts us, as we say, "in touch with" reality; touch tells us that things are *there*, not just in the mind. Touch is closer to matter, but also closer to the truth of material things, which have their being in matter; sight is closer to form. Touch is the sense of certainty. Whatever is fundamental to the sense of touch is fundamental to things themselves. This is our immediate and unshakeable perception of the world that lies before us, the world we "grasp."

In the mystery of the Incarnation, God takes delight in responding to this foundation of sanity and realism. The being of the Word is not just to be divine, spiritual, holy, but to be *man*, and therefore to be bodily, embodied, tangible. Christ tells the doubting Thomas to touch him, he tells Mary Magdalen not to touch him. St. John later writes:

That which was from the beginning, which we have heard, which we have seen with our eyes, which we have looked upon and touched with our hands, concerning the word of life—the life was made manifest, and we saw it, and testify to it, and proclaim to you the eternal life which was with the Father and was made manifest to us... (1 Jn 1:1–2)

In our Lord Jesus Christ, the God who is always and everywhere, who dwells in Light inaccessible, infinitely beyond us evanescent and confined mortals, deigns to become the *here* and *now* in flesh and blood, a body we can touch and hold on to for certain, a soul we can intimately know and love. Praised be this man, our God and Lord Jesus Christ, now and forever! "He is the head of the body, the Church; He is the beginning, the firstborn from the dead, that in all things he may hold the primacy."

ABOUT THE CONTRIBUTORS

Thomas Storck, the editor of this volume, is a member of the editorial board of *The Chesterton Review* and a contributing editor of *New Oxford Review*. He has a Bachelor of Arts from Kenyon College and a Master of Arts from St. John's College, Santa Fe. He is the author of five books and most recently translator of Cardinal Louis Billot's *Liberalism, A Critique of Its Basic Principles and Various Forms*. Many of his essays and articles may be found on the website, www.thomasstorck.org

Pater Edmund Waldstein, O. Cist., is a monk of the Cistercian Abbey of Stift Heiligenkreuz in Austria, adjunct lecturer in moral theology at the Abbey's major seminary, and parish priest of Gaaden. He studied at Thomas Aquinas College in California, at Heiligenkreuz, and at the University of Vienna. He edits thejosias.com, a website on Catholic social teaching and political philosophy.

Michael Storck studied philosophy and classics at Christendom College, and earned a Ph.D. in philosophy at The Catholic University of America. He has taught at Magdalen College in Warner, NH, and Ohio Dominican University in Columbus, OH. He currently lives in Ohio with his wife and eight children.

Susan Waldstein has an S. T. D. from the University of Fribourg in Switzerland. After finishing thirty years of homeschooling their eight children, she now teaches theology with her husband Michael at Franciscan University of Steubenville. She writes and speaks on the interface of natural science, philosophy of nature, and theology.

Christopher Shannon, Ph.D., is associate professor of history at Christendom College. He is the author of several books, including *The Past as Pilgrimage: Narrative, Tradition and the Renewal of Catholic History* (co-authored with Christopher O. Blum).

Christopher Zehnder earned his bachelor of arts degree from Thomas Aquinas College in Santa Paula, California, and his master's in theology from Holy Apostles College and Seminary in Cromwell, Connecticut. He is the general editor for the Catholic Textbook Project and written four of the books in its history series. In addition, Mr. Zehnder has authored two historical novels on the German Reformation, edited two monthlies, and written for various publications on historical, political, and theological subjects. Since 2017, he and his wife, Katherine, with their children have taken refuge in Central Ohio from drought and fires in their native state, California.

David Clayton is an internationally known artist, teacher, author, composer, and broadcaster. He moved to the US from his native England in 2009. A graduate of Oxford University, he is Provost and a founding faculty member of a new Catholic university www.Pontifex.University. Clayton designed and implemented Pontifex's Master of Sacred Arts program, a formation for all creatives based upon that given to great artists of the past. His blog and podcast are at thewayofbeauty. org. His books include *Painting the Nude — The Theology of the Body and the Representation of Man in Christian Art*, *The Way of Beauty*, and *The Vision for You — How to Discover the Life You Were Made For*. He also plays Appalachian-style old-time clawhammer banjo.

Dr. Peter Kwasniewski, Thomistic theologian, liturgical scholar, and choral composer, is a graduate of Thomas Aquinas College and The Catholic University of America. He has taught for the International Theological Institute in Austria, the Franciscan University of Steubenville's Austria Program, and Wyoming Catholic College, which he helped establish in 2006. He writes regularly for blogs, magazines, and newspapers, and has published nine books, five of which concern traditional Catholicism. Visit his website at www. peterkwasniewski.com